SMART
WEDDING

Aleisha McCormack

ALEISHA MCCORMACK is a bride who successfully pulled off her big day under a budget. She's a stand up comedian, writer and television presenter and has written for many popular Australian comedy television programs. She loves DIY projects and barters on a regular basis. For more tips follow Aleisha's Pinterest page: http://www.pinterest.com/leishamccormack/

Published by:
Wilkinson Publishing Pty Ltd
ACN 006 042 173
Level 4, 2 Collins St Melbourne, Victoria, Australia 3000
Ph: +61 3 9654 5446
www.wilkinsonpublishing.com.au

International distribution by Pineapple Media Limited (wwwpineapple-media.com)   ISSN 2202-5782

Copyright © 2014

All rights reserved. No part of this publication may be reproduced, stored in a retrieval system or transmitted in any form by any means without the prior permission of the copyright owner. Enquiries should be made to the publisher.

Every effort has been made to ensure that this book is free from error or omissions. However, the Publisher, the Author, the Editor or their respective employees or agents, shall not accept responsibility for injury, loss or damage occasioned to any person acting or refraining from action as a result of material in this book whether or not such injury, loss or damage is in any way due to any negligent act or omission, breach of duty or default on the part of the Publisher, the Author, the Editor, or their respective employees or agents.

The Author, the Publisher, the Editor and their respective employees or agents do not accept any responsibility for the actions of any person - actions which are related in any way to information contained in this book.

National Library of Australia Cataloguing-in-Publication data:

Author:	McCormack, Aleisha, author
Title:	Smart wedding : cut through hype & hidden costs / Aleisha McCormack.
ISBN:	9781922178473 (paperback)
Subjects:	Weddings--Planning--Economic aspects. Weddings--Costs.
Dewey Number:	392.5
Layout Design:	Tango Media Pty Ltd
Cover Design:	Tango Media Pty Ltd

Photos and illustrations by agreement with international agencies, photographers and illustrators including Getty and iStock.

Contents

Congratulations you're engaged ... credit card please 4
Budgeting — keep it low and aim high 7
How to plan a wedding without using the word 'wedding' 11
Guest List 13
Hired help 17
App'ily ever after 21
The Ceremony 22
Pick a venue ... any venue 24
A piece of cake 38
Flowers 42
Let's get busy: decorations 47
Wedding magazines 56
Buying an engagement ring and wedding band; how to spot a good diamond 57
Don't wear that 59
Shoes 74
Hair & Make up 77
Ladies and Gents, brideslaves and groomsmen 80
DIY (without doing it yourself) 86
Happy snaps 90
Videography 94
The business end: Invitations 96
Personalised web pages 104
Hens night & Bucks nights 106
Bridal showers and cellar parties (aka free stuff) 109
Wedding day Transport 112
Let me entertain you 115
Bonbonniere 119
Gimme gimme gimme ... gifts and honeymoon 122
Go forth and conquer 126

Congratulations
YOU'RE ENGAGED

... CREDIT CARD PLEASE

*Well done you!
It feels good, yeah?
A bit panicked?
Sure, of course you are.*

Hopefully by now you've bathed in the just-engaged attention ... milk that, it feels good. You've got a ring on it, if that's your thing, and you're feeling relief that you no longer have to respond to the often grating, "**So when are you getting married?**" question.

Now you've got that out of the way, let's start the insanity.

Aside from committing yourself to another person for the rest of your life (well, half of you ... sorry I'm a realist) many of you have also committed to organising the most expensive party of your life. Because that's what a wedding is. A really, really expensive party. On average couples spend between $25,000 and **$40,000** on a wedding (£16- 25,000).

$40,000 (£25,000) for a six-hour party?! For reals.

Unless you're Beyoncé and your fiancé is Jay-Z, that's a lot of money; but thousands of sane, non-millionaire couples pay just that, often going into debt and hammering credit cards, all for their dream wedding day.

Having a wedding on a budget doesn't have to equate to a dry bar and guests bringing a plate, there are many subtle and creative tactics to shave costs and add an extra layer of individuality to your big day.

Planning a wedding should be memorable, special and fun, after all it is supposed to be the "happiest day of your life". Unfortunately for many couples the financial burden of planning a wedding can be vexing, with a quarter of couples putting some of the costs on their credit card and even taking out personal loans.

Standard hospitality and transport service prices, with the addition of the magic "wedding" word are a ticket to inflation. "Wedding flowers", "Wedding cars", and "Wedding cake" equal money, money, money for many vendors. It's a rip off. Often the desire to have the "perfect day" overshadows cost. People go mental, spending money that they just don't have.

Finding discounts in the world of weddings isn't easy, but I'm going to show you that it can be done ... because I did it. My husband and I planned our big day for under $10,000 (£6,300). We didn't long for anything and few sacrifices were made.

It doesn't make you cheap for wanting to cut costs and there are many ways, both small and large, to shave the dollars off the overall bill. In the wedding business the saying *you get what you pay for* isn't necessarily true. This book offers hundreds of useful tips and links to vendors and discount suppliers worldwide. It's easy to save money and still have the wedding of your dreams, you just have to be organised, prepared to shop around and do your research, and most importantly be super stringent – it's your wedding and your money.

The most important key to sticking to a wedding budget is, wait for it ... *having a budget*. It may be obvious but you would be surprised at how many couples avoid tracking their costs and spending. Hey, it's like those pesky credit card bills. If you don't open the envelope it doesn't exist, right? Yeah until the debt collector comes knocking. With weddings, if you don't add up all of those small (but substantial) costs then it doesn't count, right? No way José.

Knowing exactly how much money you have to spend and allocating costs prior to organising will not only help you set limits, it will also ensure you drive a hard bargain and negotiate. Have you been to Asia on holidays? Bartered for a pair of sunglasses or a sarong with a street vendor? It's a game. It's the same with weddings; set your price and be prepared to walk away.

The wedding industry is a feisty beast. Vendors and venues, caterers and cake makers, are all out to get maximum dollars in their pockets.

Planning a wedding is emotive. It's a day about celebrating feelings. Some have fantasised about their *dream day* since preschool. These super-charged emotions and expectations can often mar budgetary constraints and create a hazy cloud of want, no matter what the cost.

When planning a wedding, best to put your business heels on, temporarily suppress those *I'll pay anything for my dream day* feelings, do your research and play hardball. You *can* have your dream wedding ... without being Beyoncé.

Dear friend,

We would like to invite you to our wedding.

It will probably look like every other wedding you have been to. It will go for 6 hours. With 120 guests we won't get much time to talk to you. During cocktail hour, we'll catch your eye and wave at you from across the room. You will mouth "congratulations" while crunching on an $8 bag of sugar-coated almond bonbonerie.

Sara will wear a dress worth more than our car (that she'll "promise" to sell after the wedding, but it will sit in our spare room cupboard for the next decade). Peter will hire an ill-fitting suit. We will pay twice the amount of money for your meal than you would in a Michelin star restaurant. You will drink catering wine (a $12 bottle that we paid $50 for) and we will be in debt for the next 7 years paying it all off. We hope you buy us a returnable gift so after the wedding we can cash it in to cover our rent.

Looking forward to seeing you there,

Peter and Sara

BUDGETING

keep it low and aim high

STOP.
*I know you're excited.
I know you're engaged and you want to begin planning the wedding.*

I know you want to buy things. I know you have been dreaming about this your WHOLE life, blah blah blah, BUT let's just all take a second to breathe.

Ok.

Before you do anything … and I mean anything … before you enter a dress shop or confer with a caterer … first things first.

Money.

How much have you got and **how much do you want to spend?**

Let's not be shy or bashful, I am talking real figures here, not "If we won the lottery", or "If we sold a kidney each", or "If I do an extra forty-six shifts at work", I mean what is the realistic figure that you can afford without going into debt or having to obtain the services of a loan shark?

No matter what your final budget is, the quickest way to get a handle on costs is to be honest with yourself about what you can spend. Not what you'd like to spend but

SMART WEDDING 7

Take Note!

Create a notebook or folder to collect quotes and keep track of receipts. Record all costs, no matter how big or small that are incurred when planning the wedding so as to create an accurate record of spending.

A budget can only be kept when you're honest and organised.

As my personal trainer says, "It's the honesty system, and you're only cheating yourself."

what is realistic. Being truthful about your budget isn't saying you have to give up on what you really want; it's the first step in deciding what is really important to you for the day and which areas you can cut back in and get a bit creative with.

I used to live in a bit of a money dreamland. A land where something marvellous was always going to come along and save my arse; a money tree, a spot on *Deal or No Deal*, a long lost dead relative that would leave me a country estate and shares in Apple that they purchased in 1984. I wasn't irresponsible, I just wasn't aware. In my late twenties I woke up from

When you have decided on your final budget, set that as a cap and do not go over it.

SMART WEDDING

my money haze and decided to stop being a debt slave who got palpitations every time the credit card bill arrived. It took me a while but I dug myself out of that debt and I never want to go back to that way of living again.

When we got engaged, Rich and I set up a new savings account. We decided that $10,000 (£6,300) was the absolute maximum that we could afford to spend on our wedding. Sure, we could have saved up and spent more but when it came to it, not wanting to get a loan and give up holidays and dinners out for the next five years, we thought $10,000 was realistic. We had a year to save and organise.

When you have decided on your final budget, set that as a cap and do not go over it. The easiest way to do that is to separate wedding money and everyday money. If your budget is $15,000 (£9,500), create a wedding bank account and only pay for wedding costs from that account. Don't dip into your everyday money. It's easy to spend a bit here and a bit there and blow the budget completely. There are a plethora of online savings accounts that incur minimal, if any, fees and are convenient for keeping track of spending online.

Talk with each other about your expectations for the day. What are your non-negotiables? When you imagine your wedding what do you see? Is it a big lavish party? Is it a cultural celebration? Is it about great food and wine? What would you exchange or let go in order to make this day really wonderful?

For example, if your dream dress is $6,000 (£3,500) and your total wedding budget is $10,000 (£6,500), then the reception is going to be pretty sparse or you need pick another dress. There are big decisions and it's only the beginning.

Too often weddings are marketed as the bride's day, but it takes two to tango and two to get married. If your future husband/wife doesn't seem as enthralled by the minute details of the day, get them involved. Talk about your expectations of the day and ask about theirs. If they don't seem jazzed about the turquoise and pink colour scheme it might be because they secretly loathe it.

Reality TV shows focus on psycho brides lamenting about **THEIR DAY** and their moment, spewing demands and acting like total a-holes to anyone who dare stand in their way. Don't be that person. I say this because instead of reminiscing about your

SMART WEDDING

gorgeous ceremony and amazing speeches, if you act like a jerk, your guests, family and friends will instead remember the bride's (or groom's) snippy 'tude' and ungracious behaviour. That's not what it's all about and if it is to you, then I suggest you put down the book and apply to be on a reality TV show, because you might be just what they're after.

BUDGET BASICS

The easiest way to keep a budget is to keep it simple. Allocate funds for each category below. Having a 10% contingency fund for additional expenses will save you from having to make choices on the fly or having to borrow money or sacrifice things that you really want to include in your wedding. If you don't spend it, well then good for you! That's extra money in your pocket.

$ _____ Clothing and Accessories (Bride, Groom and attendants)
$ _____ Photography/Videography
$ _____ Venue hire
$ _____ Reception catering
$ _____ Celebrant
$ _____ Stationery
$ _____ Cake
$ _____ Flowers
$ _____ Honeymoon
$ _____ Music & Entertainment
$ _____ Miscellaneous (contingency)

smart STEPS

✸ Remember it's a BIG day but it's only ONE day.

✸ Set a budget and stick to it.

✸ Avoid going into debt.

✸ Don't make big decisions under duress.

✸ Open a wedding bank account and only use that money for the wedding.

✸ Keep track of spending with a notebook or spread sheet … NO CHEATING.

Talk with each other about your expectations for the day. What are your non-negotiables?

How to plan a wedding
without using the word
WEDDING

An interesting and often frustrating exercise when budgeting for a wedding is comparing the cost of a non-wedding function, like a birthday or anniversary party to a wedding reception. On paper there is really no difference between these events but the wedding industry doesn't see it that way.

For example, let's take a 30th birthday party for 100 guests with all food and beverages to be supplied by the vendor. I approached a local golf club with a request for a quotation. They offered three function packages. The mid range package was $79 (£50) per head, which included a two-course meal and four-hour all-inclusive beverage package; "outside cake" could be brought on to the premises and the beverage package could be extended at an extra cost. They would decorate the room for no additional charge.

Later I approached the same golf club, but this time using the word **wedding**. I was quoted $129 (£80) per head. The food and beverage allocation was identical to the 30th birthday party but instead this package did not include decorations (and they would be charging a decorating fee, even if we were to do our own decorating), a cleaning fee and finally a charge to bring in an outside cake. **The word wedding added $50 (£30) per head to the total cost** plus the additional fees and services, which, when tallied, has increased my hypothetical function cost by $4,000 (£2,500).

So what are the options when planning your wedding? Of course it would be difficult and possibly fraudulent to plan a 30th birthday party with a venue and then rock up in a white dress with a bridal party, but there's nothing wrong with doing your research.

Follow the same exercise as I did. Call and inquire with vendors without using the 'W' word, (it can be hard!) then call again and ask about their wedding quotations. If the price is vastly different call them out on it.

- How is a **wedding** buffet any different to a **birthday** buffet?
- Why are we being charged **extra money** for cleaning?
- Why can I bring my own birthday cake but **not a wedding cake**?

smart STEPS

✷ Inquire with potential venues about the price difference between a 'normal' event and a wedding.

✷ If there is a price difference, ask the vendor to explain the difference in service.

✷ Avoid mentioning that it is a wedding that you are planning.

✷ Get everything in writing.

- Why is the wine suddenly **more expensive**?
- Is it cheaper to hold your event on a **Sunday** or **weekday**?

This exercise can be used throughout your wedding planning. Of course some venues and vendors do add special services to their packages. I'm not trying to suggest that they are all dishonest ... just most of them.

GUEST LIST

Have you ever felt guilty for being a guest at a wedding? An obligation guest? As a co-worker, uni-friend, second cousin? I know I have. Me being at their wedding probably cost them $150 (£100), sure I had a fab time but I saw them for three minutes on the day, drank all their champagne and I haven't seen them since. Guilt trip much?

It is always difficult creating a guest list for any event let alone a wedding. There's a lot of pressure in making this list, which usually focuses around the following; emotional blackmail, people from the past and cousins. Wedding guest lists are 'worlds collide' at their best and worst. You've got people attending that have never met each other, people that have and may not get along and those tricky few … people who expect an invitation, even though they don't deserve one.

In the end it comes down to:
✦ How much **money** do you have?
✦ How **many people** can the venue fit?
✦ Who's **in**?
✦ Who's **out**?
✦ What are your **obligations**?

Like your budget, with guest list and numbers you're going to need to set clear goals and guidelines.

What is your absolute maximum number of guests?

This is always fun … do you first work out your guest list and then your budget, or do you find a venue, work out the pricing and then the guest list?

I suggest, early on, preferably the same time you calculate your budget, you sit down together and write a first draft, including people who absolutely must be invited, such as immediate family and close friends. Next on the list are friends, co-workers and distant relatives.

Now you have a clear first draft list.

Unless money is no option or you are having a large wedding venue, cutting the list is inevitable. Make an *A* and a *B* List; with *A* the 'must invite' list and *B* the 'maybe but not vital to invite' list.

Are there names on the list that you don't recognise or people that you hardly know? Maybe they are suggestions from parents and in-laws. If you are paying for and organising your wedding, then it is totally up to you who is invited. If parents are contributing to the cost, then you might have some negotiating to do.

Talk to your parents about why it is important to them that these 'extra' guests attend. Is it a keeping up with the Joneses situation? Do they want to show you off? That's nice but not at $300 (£190), per couple. If that's the case, offer to send them a photo and card or invite them to the ceremony only (controversial I know, but it

---

Like your budget, with guest list numbers you're going to need to set clear goals and guidelines. What is your absolute maximum number of guests?

won't cost you anything). Guest lists get out of hand when other people are involved. Don't invite anyone (I said **ANYONE**) because you feel you have to. Don't invite anyone you have to pretend to be happy to see.

That is rubbish.

Your wedding day is the one-day you shouldn't have to fake smile at **ALL**.

Like a wardrobe clean out, if you haven't seen a friend in years, cut them free. If you don't know their kids' names or have their current address, forget it. Just because you re-kindled a friendship on Facebook doesn't mean they get to come to your wedding.

The best advice we were given when planning our invite list was that **wedding guests should be people that you want in your future, not just your past**. After hearing that, we cut our list from 86 to 56. We liked the 30 people, no doubt, but some were friends of friends, old uni friends who we hadn't met up with in over three years and the most debatable move was not inviting partners of friends and cousins who we had never met. OK, I know this one is tricky. If they are so important to you (and live in the same country) then why haven't you met them? Yes there are alternatives when it comes to this rule, I'll leave it up to your discretion. But seriously if your second cousin has a new boyfriend that she just met but thinks 'he's the one'… well let them have their third date at a restaurant, not at your wedding.

Co-workers can be problematic. You are around them all of the time, they hear about your plans, but again they are people you have been put with, not by choice but by association. Would you be their friend if you weren't working with them? If you left work next week, would you stay in touch? Set a precedent, perhaps if you have no association with them outside work hours, then no invitation. Don't invite the whole office just because you feel guilty. If you are friends with Jane from Accounts but secretly loathe everyone else, just invite her and forget the rest. You'll probably get a promotion soon or move to a better company.

The same theory goes for **bridesmaids and groomsmen**. Don't have six just because you don't want to leave someone out. Weddings aren't about onus. They are about you and your partner ... and cake. If you can't cut your bridesmaids list down, just pick one friend to be your maid of honour and give the other five special jobs at the wedding, like doing a reading or looking after weird aunty Val. This way they still feel included but you save all the dramas and any opportunity for one of the friends that has been left out to create a nightmare and make the day that is 'all about you' about them. Trust me; one out of three bridesmaids will do this. **FACT**.

As with all big decisions, the guest list should be worked on **together** to save any unnecessary arguments. Remember, you are a team, work together. You can do it. I believe in you.

smart STEPS

* Fix your budget before creating your guest list.
* Create an A and B list.
* Don't invite people out of obligation.
* Guests should be in your future and not just from your past.
* Don't invite anyone that you have to pretend to be happy around.

Wedding guests should be people that you want in your future, not just your past.

16   SMART WEDDING

Hired HELP

I like organising, planning, making lists, colour coding lists, worrying about lists, bartering, schmoozing and getting a job done. Many people do not like doing the aforementioned things.

Hiring a wedding planner or supervisor for the day may seem like something only rich people do but you would be surprised at the advantages that the right person can bring. Experienced wedding planners come with a pre-existing vendor list, people that they work with regularly, trust and rely on. **Their business is making sure your wedding goes to plan.** They panic when the flowers don't show up on the morning of the wedding, not you. If the icing on the cake is green instead of white or there are no chairs for your guests to sit on during the ceremony, it's their

SMART WEDDING 17

problem to fix … that's what you pay them for. Wedding planners can also;

+ **Add details** to the day that you might have missed (or not even thought of),
+ give you an **alternative perspective** and keep you up-to-date on current and future wedding trends,
+ produce **design elements** to create a personalised look,
+ **coordinate** the florist, caterer, printers, graphic designers, transport and any other additional vendors,
+ **design** table settings and decor, lighting and other audiovisual details, and
+ advise on possible **entertainment**.

Experienced wedding planners should know everyone in the business, what's new, who sucks, where someone got food poisoning last week and who drives a hard bargain. They should be able to do everything from helping you find the ideal wedding ceremony location to the extra little touches you may not have considered. They should use this prowess, their contacts and knowledge to get you the best prices and those extra special inclusions. Any vendors they recommend should always be within your limitations. They should not be receiving kickbacks from vendors for your business.

So what are wedding coordinators generally paid?

Each coordinator will charge their own fees but generally there are three categories of service fees.

Set fee, fixed price
Regardless of the size of your wedding or your budget a set fee is negotiated.

By the hour
The 'pay as you go' system might seem initially affordable but the more time the coordinator clocks up the more money you pay. This option can work though if you only require them for the day of your wedding.

Percentage
Those with bigger budgets will pay more, while people with smaller budgets pay less. Some consultants ask for up to 15% of the wedding budget. If you choose this option, negotiate a price cap, especially if your budget gets out of hand (which it won't if you follow the rules!).

If hiring a wedding coordinator is something that you are considering, it may seem obvious to say but don't employ the first person you meet. Interview a few coordinators, test the field and snoop around. Ask for examples of weddings that they have arranged with similar budgets to yours. Treat it like a job interview (**BECAUSE IT IS**).

If employing a wedding coordinator for the full planning of the wedding isn't an option for you financially, or if you don't think you need the extra help, another

Questions for Wedding Planners

- ☐ Are they certified and if not have they completed any event management courses?
- ☐ What are some of the challenges they have faced? Throw some hypotheticals at them on the spot.
- ☐ Can they work with your budget? Is it realistic?
- ☐ What are some of the ways they would suggest to save money and still have the best day ever?
- ☐ How open are they to your wants and needs?
- ☐ How much time do they devote to planning your wedding?
- ☐ Can you contact them anytime?
- ☐ What if you don't like their suppliers?
- ☐ Will they use your preferred suppliers or are they contractually obliged to use their own?
- ☐ Are they affiliated with any venues? (watch out for this)

option is hiring a day-of-the-wedding coordinator. On your wedding day, both you and your partner are going to be pulled in a million directions. You'll want to relax and get ready, and everyone will be asking you a million questions. And that's just before the ceremony starts.

Wedding planners can help you avoid this chaos by:

- ✦ **Meeting vendors** and deliveries, and handling any no-shows,
- ✦ solving any last-minute **emergencies**,
- ✦ **setting up** and checking the ceremony and reception spaces and dealing with any weather issues e.g. moving an outdoor ceremony if it is raining,
- ✦ making sure that the wedding party is running to **schedule** and in the right places at the right time,
- ✦ **coordinating** the reception timeline with venue, caterers, entertainment and MCs,
- ✦ collecting all of your **personal items**, wedding gifts, leftover wedding cake and making sure they get back to you safely,
- ✦ **returning all rentals** and borrowed items and signing off all suppliers' pick ups, and
- ✦ ensuring that the space is left clean and that your **deposits are returned**.

If you are thinking of using a 'day-of' coordinator, you should treat them like a full time wedding coordinator, interview and meet with them at least a month in advance from the wedding. You should communicate all details and contacts with as much lead time as possible to ensure that the coordinator can personally contact them and confirm that all of your suppliers are on track. Also make sure to meet with them

SMART WEDDING   19

to go over the plan for the day. A good coordinator will have a schedule document; sometimes called a call sheet, that is a rundown of the day, from when the bride and groom gets out of bed to when they leave for their honeymoon.

If a hired wedding coordinator isn't on the cards for your big day, don't worry. You have a free army of people that are emotionally obliged to help you out … your family and friends! Use them if you dare and allocate, allocate, allocate!

Weddings are huge events to organise and even if you know exactly what you want and you think you can handle it, don't be too proud (or mental) to not take on the help of others to get the job done, especially in the weeks leading up to the big day. You don't want to be super stressed and on the edge of a flip out by the time the wedding day comes along. No matter how small the job; whether it is picking up flowers or dropping off dry cleaning, take the opportunity to assign people with jobs. Create a spreadsheet or a shared document, which you can email to family and friends. Ask for their availability and be clear about what you need them to do. It's better to over than under explain, and get them to confirm their availability.

If you are looking for an easy to use shareable document and spreadsheet system, Google docs have launched **https://www.google.com/weddings/**. It's a free, time-saving system where you can collaborate with your bridal party on guest lists, schedules, addresses, and more. The all-in-one wedding planner includes ready to use documents with tabs from all aspects of the budget and lists needed for planning your wedding. You can access and edit your planning documents from the bridal shop, bakery or pretty much anywhere that you can get online. That way everyone involved can see real time schedules etc, without you having to email them every time a detail is changed or amended.

smart STEPS

✱ Ask to see examples of previous weddings the coordinator has helped plan.

✱ Ask for references from the coordinator.

✱ Hire a 'day of' coordinator to assist you on the wedding day.

✱ Use a shareable document system to keep up to date with plans, schedules and contacts.

✱ If you aren't using a wedding planner, allocate jobs to friends and family.

APP'ILY ever after...

If you like technology and have an iPhone or Android, then embrace all of the apps available for planning and capturing ideas for your wedding day. It's like a little magic wedding slave in your pocket or purse.

Magazines such as *Bride* and *The Knot* have their own apps featuring galleries upon galleries of dresses and accessories, as well as planning tools to use. You can save, capture and pop your head on lots of different dresses.

There are **apps for seating plans** ('Seating Planner+'), **flowers** ('Wedding Flowers Moodboard'), and for **music**, like 'Fun Wedding', which provides song selections in categories and downloadable lists for your DJ.

'Pinterest' and **'Wedding Gawker'** are both fab for creative inspiration, with both apps featuring real life wedding photos, DIY ideas and direct links to suppliers and vendors worldwide.

One thing I've noticed at weddings is that people are snapping away on the iPhones and Androids all day but I wondered if the bride and groom ever get to see all of those candid shots. My favourite new wedding app does just that. It's called 'Wedding party' and it's free. **'Wedding Party' allows guests to share photos** and anecdotes as they capture them during a wedding, making it fun and easy for guests to contribute to your wedding album. You can download free customised instruction place cards for your wedding day to help guests download the app and then you instantly get all your wedding photos in one album. It also creates a timeline. **Bam.**

SMART WEDDING   21

The CEREMONY

Before making any decisions about venues and the reception, you have to book the main event, the ceremony. You've got two options here: a civil ceremony, generally a non-religious service conducted by a civil celebrant, or a religious ceremony, usually held in a church, temple or synagogue etc. I was always warned to avoid talking about politics or religion … a warning I often ignore but I will say; you know what you believe in, what's important to you, your spiritual requirements and traditions.

It is entirely a personal choice, but rarely are our choices ever free. Whether your ceremony is in a church or a park, there are always fees to be paid. Staff, utilities, the celebrant or minister's fees (which can sometimes be a donation, and for the canny couple can be tax deductible), church or hall hire and 'floral donations' are common charges associated with the ceremony.

It's a chicken and the egg scenario when it comes to matching the **availability** of a **reception venue** and your **ceremony venue** (if they are separate locations). Which is more important to you? If one isn't available, do you change the other location?

✦ If you are marrying in a church, is there any pre-wedding **counselling** required?
✦ Can you meet in advance for a **rehearsal**?
✦ An obvious first question for an officiant is – **are they licensed** to perform your marriage service?
✦ Can you **write your own vows**? (Often church services are un-editable, while civil ceremonies are largely, except for the mandatory legal declarations, your call).
✦ How early is the venue/location available for **decoration**?
✦ Do you need to **pack anything up** post ceremony?
✦ Do you need to **hire additional** microphones or PA equipment?
✦ If outside, is there a rainy day **contingency** plan?

If you were considering a **destination wedding**, I would suggest that you investigate the legalities and validity of the marriage license and if after the service you will be considered legally married in your home country. Some countries require you to apply for a marriage license up to a month prior to the wedding, which is often an impossible task. A solution is to have a quickie, at home, town hall service to legalise your marriage and a civil 'for show' ceremony at the destination. If you are eloping, talk to a wedding coordinator at your destination who should have the information in regards to timing and license applications.

> *Staff, utilities, the celebrant or minister's fees, church or hall hire and 'floral donations' are common charges associated with the ceremony.*

SMART WEDDING

Pick a venue ...
ANY VENUE

Weddings can take shape in many different ways ... formal, traditional, religious, casual, huge, minimalistic, vintage inspired, Star Wars themed ... the list is long.

The right choice in wedding venue will not only make your day fab to the max but it can also save you thousands of dollars. Think laterally when beginning your search. It doesn't have to be a slapdash backyard occasion to be cost effective.

Self contained venues, where you can hold both the ceremony and reception are excellent for cutting back on transport costs. You won't have to pay for wedding cars and guest buses between venues and you can also avoid having to double up on ceremony fees that are charged by parks, gardens, beaches and churches. Finding a location for post-ceremony photographs while your guests enjoy a drink and canapés, **without that long break** is also a real winner. I once attended a wedding that had a three-hour interval between the ceremony and reception … THREE HOURS … I had time to watch *The Godfather Part II*, redo my hair AND eat the contents of my mini bar. Ridiculous.

After you have locked in your budget, the next step is to choose a venue and date. The time of the year that you plan to hold your wedding will affect the overall cost and lead-time. Spring is the most popular time to get hitched so unless you are getting married at home or at a private venue, my advice would be to try and avoid it at all costs. **Peak wedding time is like kryptonite;** when it's busy your bargaining superpowers diminish. Vendors don't work for your business because they know the next suckers are just around the corner.

Think resourcefully, if you have your heart set on a venue that is out of your budget in peak wedding time, enquire about what deals are available during the low season. You will be surprised at how many venues will work for your business when they really need it. Remember if you don't ask, they will **not** offer.

When looking at venues, imagine what sort of mood you want to create on your wedding day. Do you envisage a romantic, classic service in a ballroom decorated with roses, a string quintet and champagne? (Posh!) Or a barefoot beach wedding with fire drums, cocktails and a calypso band? An inner city warehouse adorned with origami flowers and tea lights? Finding a location that can work with what you imagine is the first step in making it happen. Be realistic though, an empty art gallery is a blank canvas but someone has to decorate it and make it awesome. Have you the time? Have you the skills? If not, can you afford to pay someone who does?

Think resourcefully, if you have your heart set on a venue that is out of your budget in peak wedding time, enquire about what deals are available during the low season.

SMART WEDDING   25

What sort of **vibe** do you want your wedding day to have? Will the reception be filled with dancing and laughter? If so is there somewhere for this frivolity to occur? It's your job to create the atmosphere of the event by selecting the right venue. Guests will contribute to the ambience, but having a live band or a DJ when getting people up to dance makes a difference, compared to just plugging your iPod into house speakers.

How would you like the reception to run? Will you have an MC? Do you want it planned down to the last second or will it be more casual? How about decorations? What will you have to do to make the venue shine? If you aren't crafty and don't want to pay a designer to transform a trendy but sparse venue, then perhaps that isn't the location for you.

Be aware that some of the most popular wedding venues can be booked well in advance, even years in some special cases (I know, crazy).

When booking any venue, whether it is a hall, art gallery, vineyard, wedding reception centre or a marquee, make sure you are clear on what is provided in the initial hire of the venue and what is an extra charge. As always, **get it in writing**.

A common tactic used by venues (which often works) is after a couple has viewed a potential venue and pencilled in a date (without a deposit), the venue calls and advises them that another couple is interested in holding their wedding on exactly the same date and that without an immediate deposit they will lose their booking.

Weddings are emotive. **Don't be bullied.**

Questions to ask a venue before signing the contract

- ☐ How many guests can the venue accommodate?
- ☐ Are there other alternative dates available?
- ☐ Is this the best price they can offer?
- ☐ What additional extras can they include to sweeten the deal?
- ☐ Are there additional charges for staying longer than the allocated time?
- ☐ Are there any hidden fees? (Cleaning, staff etc)
- ☐ Can you bring your own cake?
- ☐ If it is a hotel, will they provide a discount for the Bridal party and guests who wish to stay at the hotel?
- ☐ How late can you play music and keep the party going?
- ☐ What are the cancellation fees?

Around eighty per cent of the time there is no other couple. Be calm, be cool, breathe and play the game. If you are one-hundred per cent committed to holding your wedding at the venue on that exact date and have read through the contract, pay the money. If not, call their bluff and beat them at their own game. Tell them that you are looking at other venues and you would like time to check the contract. If they are keen enough to invent fake couples and lie to secure your business, then you should use that to your advantage.

When holding your wedding at a function centre, hotel or specialised reception venue you have a secret weapon, **a free wedding planner**. Well, a function coordinator at least.

Your wedding planner/function manager is there to make their business look good, and your event run smoothly. Use them as much as possible; ask about recommended suppliers and local additional vendors that can help you with your day.

If you **look past traditional wedding reception venues**, country clubs and hotels, you will find that your community is filled with many potential wedding venues. Warehouses, art galleries, private homes, National Trust venues and local historical societies are options worth exploring when looking for wedding reception and ceremony locations. It's surprising how many of these venues are available to hire. Many historical and estate homes are government owned, and it is simply a matter of calling your local council or checking their website for a list of venues for hire. For example, in Tasmania, Australia, the Hobart City Council owns art galleries; historical homes, waterfront piers, halls, old timber mills, the town hall and a number of former churches. All of their venues are available to hire to the public at reasonable rates ($100 to $500 per day … £60-£320). Most venues have kitchenettes or areas where a caterer could set up a temporary kitchen.

Hiring of these locations is often not publicised but it is just a matter of contacting the council in the area of interest for a list. Keep in mind you need to **book ahead of time** with these venues as often councils run their own activities and events in these locations as well as making them available for public hire, so be prepared to book well in advance.

When hiring the above mentioned locations be mindful that you will most likely need to provide everything (tables, chairs, crockery etc, which can be arranged by an event hire company). Although you may be getting a venue for cheaper you may be adding **additional hire costs** and organising time, so remember to add these factors into your budget.

With an outdoor venue, you will need to be prepared for the possibility of bad weather. Hiring a marquee is a very popular option but not always that cheap. Marquees can only be erected on certain surfaces, and there will need to be time allocated for them to be put up and taken down. Sure, you might be saving money but you don't want to be out in a paddock at 11pm, the evening of your wedding, dismantling a marquee. Also, unlike a church hall or gallery, marquees will need to have power and water nearby for lighting and catering

Questions about the venue and staff

- ☐ Are they approachable?
- ☐ Are they willing to negotiate on your terms?
- ☐ Is the date available?
- ☐ Can you ask to read a contract?
- ☐ Are they flexible with the details of the day?
- ☐ Most significantly, can you trust this venue and staff with the planning of your wedding?

purposes. Also port-a-loos if you are away from bathrooms. Be aware of the possibility of intruders such as insects and other people. If your ceremony is taking place in a public park you may attract onlookers. Is the location near a main road? Will there be surrounding traffic noise? Of course, you will need to get permission to use any public outdoor area and possibly pay a fee to the local council.

THE RECEPTION FOOD

Being on a budget doesn't mean you have to have bland pre-packed, frozen catering. There are alternatives to the traditional meat and two veg wedding reception. A morning champagne brunch or lunch event can be far less expensive than an evening or weekend function. Some restaurants will also charge considerably less for a weekend lunchtime slot, so they can still open in the evening. Guests also drink less at lunchtime (well, some guests).

ALCOHOL AT A HOTEL OR FUNCTION CENTRE

A hotel or reception centre may suit your needs, especially if planning and managing every detail of the event isn't an option for you. Most hotels will provide you with **package deal options**, which will include everything you need to hold a function; food, beverages, staffing and venue hire. Full service wedding venues, such as function centres will provide everything you can think of, plus more. Weddings put on by these types of venues could perhaps be labelled as 'cookie cutter' but you have control. You make your day, your way. So even if you are having your reception in a hotel dining area, get busy with the décor and personalised touches!

With full-catered hospitality packages, you will be given a choice of **how many courses** you wish to be served; as well as **beverage selections**, including timed beverage packages where you pay a capped fee per head for a period of alcohol service, which can be an economical option, particularly if you know your guests are solid drinkers.

For example, you may pay $39 (£24), per guest for unlimited wine and beer for 4 hours. On average a guest in their 20s who drinks alcohol will consume 4 to 6 standard drinks at an evening wedding. So if you were to buy by the glass, a house wine at $6.50 (£4), per glass that would equal about $45 (£28). This is an economically viable option for this guest but what about Nanna and your pregnant cousin? Perhaps they will only drink a glass of champagne for the toasts? They've now lost you about $70 (£45).

Choosing a beverage package really **depends on your guest list**. Do you have pregnant guests, older people, non-drinkers, kids? That will help you decide the best package for your function.

An open bar, where guests drink for free but you pay the bill can be successful for smaller functions. You organise ahead

If you look past traditional wedding reception venues, you will find that your community is filled with many potential wedding venues.

SMART WEDDING   29

of time with the venue a figure, of say $1,000 (£650) and when, and if, the limit is reached, they let you know and you can decide whether to top it up or move on to a cash bar. This way **you are in control** of what you spend and you don't receive a nasty surprise by the way of a crazy bill at the end of the night. Once you have set your limits, stick to them. It is in the best interest of the vendor to allow your guests to buy alcohol by the glass after your allotted money has run out; this shouldn't be a negotiating point.

If you have an open bar, make sure you discuss with the venue what your guests can order. Choose cheaper or mid-range selections of wines, such as Prosecco (Italian sparkling wine) instead of champagne, and limit the range of spirits and beer for your guests, to keep the costs down.

At our wedding, we prepared a **signature cocktail** to serve with our grazing table (which we negotiated with our caterer to prepare ourselves). 'Schnappily ever after' was a simple cocktail of peach Schnapps, peach nectar and Prosecco. We served it in little vintage milk bottles, which we later resold on ebay. We also had paper straws to match our polka dot theme. During the cocktail hour we served limited wine and beer but the cocktails were a hit and kept alcohol consumption steady during that period.

In locations such as vineyards, you are going to be pushed to find inexpensive wine and there are obviously no other options regarding bringing in alternative alcohol. That's their business! Be upfront with the venue about what you can afford and discuss and ask what has worked with previous functions that they have managed.

If you do have a set limit on the bar, choose a friend or parent to be the go-to person for the venue to discuss money with. Neither the Bride nor Groom should have to think about money or credit cards during their celebration.

If your venue is self-catering, or doesn't serve alcohol but will let you supply your own, wholesale deals, especially on the Internet, are abundant. One of the most reliable cost savings advantages is purchasing cleanskin and wholesale wine. Cleanskin wine outlets are popping up all over the place and often stock premium wines for 30-50% off the original labelled price. You can **personalise wine labels**, create your own 'vineyard for the day' or apply a photo of the happy couple using an easy print at home label.

Many boutique vineyards also sell leftover stock to cleanskins outlets and

quite often such stores are willing to negotiate a bulk discount. You can but ask! There is a multitude of alcohol wholesale clubs and discount companies on the Internet who also offer deals on beer and bulk spirits.

When buying alcohol in bulk, try and negotiate a **return policy**. If you end up buying too much, pre-arrange the return of unused alcohol. It's surprising how many smaller retailers and large companies such as Costco and supermarket chains provide this option as long as you keep the receipt and the original packaging is still intact.

FOOD AT A HOTEL OR FUNCTION CENTRE

As with alcohol, venues will offer a range of choices when it comes to food service, most quoting a price per head. Quotes can include a pre dinner cocktail service with canapés, a main meal, buffet and dessert. The more complicated and individualised, the more expensive it gets.

COCKTAIL RECEPTIONS

A cocktail reception can be very social and if you fancy walking around and mingling with your guests, not to mention getting everyone on the dance floor sooner rather than later, this may be a good option.

This type of reception can also be **rather economical**.

Cocktail receptions don't necessarily mean that your guests will go home hungry as there are many substantial dishes that can be served 'cocktail style'. Talk to your venue (or caterer) about what they recommend. Most venues will offer a sample menu and a tasting once you have confirmed your booking with them … don't miss out on this opportunity to try the food and make suggestions about what you like and don't like.

Often during cocktail receptions, couples choose to serve canapés during the first 90 minutes of the reception and then follow it by a self-serve dessert table or sweet buffet, which can include a range of sweet treats from mini cakes and ice-cream cones (if you can keep them cold), to chocolate fountains, macaroons and any number of lollies in all sorts of colours and flavours. Using the wedding cake as the centrepiece of the dessert table is also a fabulous idea.

We had Cake Ink create a marvellous three-tier (two fake tier… more about that later) cake and our friend who ran a boutique baking company made a selection of bite-sized treats to complete our **dessert table**. It was the focal point of the room and guests couldn't wait to get stuck into it. We also included small Chinese takeaway boxes for guests to take home a selection of goodies instead of bonbonniere.

SMART WEDDING

If you are getting married in summer, try a DIY ice cream sundae bar … you can hire a soft serve machine for a reasonable price then create your own selection of fresh fruit, sprinkles, fudges and condiments for decorations. Guests love to get involved and this is a cheap and easy way to personalise a dessert bar.

For more **substantial food**, but keeping within the cocktail reception boundaries, set up a range of self-service food stations (managed and maintained by venue staff). Noodle bars, paella, burger or curry stations are a way to add diversity to the food and cut out table service.

Just because a wedding reception is cocktail in style doesn't mean it has to forgo the traditional formalities such as speeches, cake cutting and the couple's first dance. Having said that, if you're opting for a cocktail function because you want to avoid the conventional customs, go nuts!

Cocktail receptions may be held during the afternoon, particularly if you're marrying in a garden or seaside setting. More commonly they are held indoors during the evening but usually limited to **no more than 4 hours** out of consideration for guest's feet! If you plan on raging on late into the night, provide additional seating. The traditional ratio is to have enough seats for about a third of your guests, made up of bar stools, regular seats and armchairs or couches scattered around. Nanna and your stiletto-wearing friends will thank you!

SHARED TABLES

Something very hip and clever is the **grazing table/shared platter** reception. (Please note, I'm claiming it as hip because we had one!)

If a cocktail reception feels a little casual and you wish to have your guests seated at the reception, you can avoid the often-boring alternate drop food option by asking your caterer about shared plates. A homely and generous way to serve food (but still **less expensive** and **more inventive** than giving everyone the same dish) is with platters. Each table can have a selection of vegetables, salads and breads, or antipasto platters and main meals that they can serve themselves.

One caterer I spoke to recently said that shared platters are really just 'fancy buffets' but they are also the most popular choice on their menu. Staffing is lower as they don't have to plate and deliver hundreds of meals and menus can be more exotic and inventive. Guests also feel like they are in control with portion sizes and feel like they are getting a choice, without having to line up at a buffet.

CHAMPAGNE AND CAKE RECEPTION

Head back to the sixties with the champagne and cake reception. This is

exactly what it sounds like. Instead of serving a three-course meal, make your wedding an afternoon affair with a table of gorgeous cakes and a healthy selection of champagne and wine. Gather everyone after the ceremony for a piece (or plate) of **cake(s) and toasts.** Have your reception in the garden of your ceremony venue, or even right in the same room. If you opt for this kind of reception, give your guests a heads up on the invitation … **'Champagne and cake to follow'** so that guests will know there isn't a full meal and they'll probably have to stop for a dirty burger on the way home.

This reception style is great for a couple who may have eloped but still want to celebrate with family and friends or if you don't want a nine hour, all out celebration. I've attended a wonderful champagne and cake reception that had an 'after party' at a local cocktail lounge so those who wanted to hit the dance floor and continue on could. Everyone paid for their own drinks at the after party and had a fabulous time without financially crippling the bride and groom.

'POT LUCK' WEDDING

A popular and rather old school catering option is a 'pot luck wedding'. Don't stop reading … it's not as bad as it sounds, in fact it can be rather awesome *if you do it right*.

It is truly a low budget option but can make your reception a personalised affair. The fundamentals of this idea are that the couple asks guests to cater for them. The old **'ladies please bring a plate'** option*.

You can pick a theme, like high tea, curry banquet, summer salads, seafood or Mediterranean. You simply slip a note in with the invite, to give the guests the option to help you cater.

SMART WEDDING   33

For example the note might read:

> *Our reception will celebrate the delicacies of the Mediterranean.*
>
> *_____ Please check here if you would like to bring a dish for the reception in place of a wedding gift. Call with dish suggestions please.*

By having the guests contact you beforehand, you can have control over the menu. No one is obligated to participate, but it would be interesting to see how many guests would opt for doing this and the quality of the fare (not that your wedding is my science experiment but hey!).

In Egypt, the bride's family traditionally does all the cooking for a week after the wedding, so the couple can relax.

With the correct wording, and re-plating the meals on vintage platters or the dinnerware as they come in, you could create a delicious (both to look at and eat) buffet that didn't cost you a cent. You can guarantee people will put in a monster effort and create fabulous meals. Families are competitive, especially in-laws.

Sure this isn't for everyone. It takes organisation, and may I suggest balls, but it can be done.

If you don't want to go all the way with this option, you could use this method for one course, such as the dessert table … *Guests, bring your favourite cake* is going to save you a lot of money and it will be DELICIOUS!

*BIG NOTE. Always be mindful of correct food handling procedures, heating and storing food prior to the day. Hiring a cool room or additional oven facilities is preferable to managing such an event. There is no bigger downer than all of your guests going home with salmonella instead of a bag of sugared almonds.

SELF CATERING VENUE (THE BUDGET WEDDING JACKPOT)

Finding a wedding reception venue that allows outside catering is a possible goldmine of savings. If you are lucky

Questions for a self-catering venue

- ☐ Do they have a list of preferred vendors (caterers, hire companies etc)?
- ☐ What have been some of their most successful functions?
- ☐ Can you see photos?
- ☐ Are there any specific details about the venue that you should pass on to a caterer?
- ☐ Is there a fully functioning kitchen or do you have to bring your own?
- ☐ How much set up time will they allow (very important)?
- ☐ What are the occupational health and safety restrictions (if any)?
- ☐ Do you have to supply your own public liability insurance?

enough to secure one of these gems it's imperative that early on in the process you acquire all of the necessary info about what you can and can't do on the property.

Treat the caterer as you would the function coordinator. **Bargain, bargain, bargain.** Caterers are generally smaller companies, and it's a competitive market. Often caterers are keen to service new venues, so perhaps there is a deal to be done, for example sharing photographs of your event that they can use on their website and introducing them to the venue operator for future functions.

When choosing menu options, try and select the **less labour-intensive dishes.** Canapés can be expensive but a grazing table with antipasto selection during cocktail hour can be both novel and pretty to look at.

A buffet or self-serve meal service may save you the expense of additional wait staff but can also be more expensive depending on the style of food and number of guests. A gourmet seafood buffet will be far more costly than an alternate drop main meal.

When hiring a self-catering venue, and not using a professional wedding planner, often the onus is on the couple to arrange the hire of all glasses, crockery, platters, tables, linen, chairs etc.

Try and arrange these items through the caterer, as most will have a recommended event hire supplier. Hiring these items yourself can sometimes be costly but hiring everything from one vendor gives you the advantage of **price negotiation** and **one stop delivery.** Larger hire companies will provide everything from salt and pepper shakers to amplifiers for the DJ and will deliver and pick up hire items prior to and post event.

Make note of replacement fees for broken items and check with the hire company if you are expected to return the crockery and glassware clean (which is unlikely as most companies will clean goods in-house).

Alternative wedding venues

Restaurants
Theatres
A shipboard reception
National Parks
Heritage steam trains
Heritage mansions or town halls
Private houses
Architectural icons
Zoos and wildlife parks
Golf and Country Clubs
Community centres
Libraries
Friend's backyard
Farms
Schools
Museums
Riverside BBQ
A beach
Vineyards
Universities (ask if they offer deals for alumni)
Botanical gardens

decorations and gifts, the cleanup will be taken care of by the venue. If you are in the situation of having to come back to tidy and are using a wedding planner, get them to organise a cleanup team to ensure that the hire bond is returned in full.

One disadvantage of the **DIY 'run-your-own-wedding'** option is that returning the next morning with a mop is discouraging. You have a wonderful wedding, say goodbye and then have to return to vacuum the room, fold chairs and clean. Not everyone's ideal start to the honeymoon.

Our venue was a private house, which we hired for two nights (Friday and Saturday). It slept 16 people. On the Friday, we invited our nearest and dearest to come to the property to hang out and help us set up the living room, which we transformed into a reception venue. We hired the tables and chairs, which were delivered on the Friday morning. We moved all of the furniture out of the lounge room and set up the tables, bar area and ceremony area,

The same questions can be asked of the caterer. Will they **clean the venue** after you have left or will you be expected to return the following day to pack up? If you choose to have your reception at a function venue or hotel this won't be a factor. Besides having to remove

Queen Victoria's wedding cake weighed a whopping 136kg.

which was in the courtyard of the venue. Our caterer was happy to do all of this for us, at a charge.

We opted to use our lovely **family and friends** and made them a gorgeous meal with wine and yummy things in the evening. It was a wonderful experience, we gathered friends from all of our separate worlds and they got to know each other and have a laugh before we all got up the next morning to run around like crazy, getting last minute jobs and chores done. It was a massive team effort and that made it all the more special. We all created the wedding, not a stranger (and we got to spend more money in other areas that really counted, like our amazing DJ!).

The morning after the wedding we had a big breakfast fry up and then again with the help of our guests, put the house back together again. It's not everyone's cup of tea, but it worked for us.

A **post wedding clean-up BBQ** or picnic is a tidy way to get your friends and family to bunk in and help and then reward them with lunch. It's also a good opportunity to catch up with people you might not have seen as much of as you had hoped at the event. It's true, weddings fly by and even with small groups it's hard to get around and talk to all of your guests properly. By having a **post wedding event** the following day, you can relax and get all the gossip and wonderful compliments all over again.

smart STEPS

* Don't fall for coercion tactics. Don't be pressured. Be prepared to walk away.

* Ask to see photographs and references of previous events held at the venue.

* Be prepared. Write a list of questions and requests prior to inspecting the venue.

* Get everything in writing. Do not sign a contract until you are completely satisfied with the details of the agreement.

* Do sweat the little things, especially when they might end up costing you a LOT of money ... such as, can you bring your own alcohol and cake? Are there extra cleaning fees?

* Get more bang for your buck. If you would like shared platters but the venue has never catered that option, negotiate with them. You never know until you ask.

A piece of CAKE

Mmmmmmm cake.

Cakes are important, well to me anyway. But as soon as you attach the magic 'W' word to cake, prices can triple. Having a fabulous tasting and looking cake doesn't have to break the cake bank. Wedding cakes can be labour intensive and costly, but they're also symbolic and sometimes, one of the event's biggest focal points.

It can be tempting to want to use the most popular wedding cake bakery in town. Remember that popularity means that there's a higher demand, which usually means a higher cost. Some specialist bakeries can charge **up to $4,000** (£2,500) for a decorated wedding cake. That is mental. Generally you can expect that the cost for a wedding cake will start around $3.00 (£2) per slice for traditional decorated fruitcakes, but it can be up to $5.00 (£3). Depending on how many guests you are expecting, the average cost for a wedding cake will be about $300 to $700 (£190-450). The key is to **find a bakery** that **doesn't specialise in wedding cakes.**

Aside from the obvious, and dare I say risqué option of making the cake yourself, which can be an unnecessary stress so close to the day, there are plenty of other options to escape the costs of the traditionally expensive and often exuberantly priced wedding cakes.

Before ordering anything, think about **how many people** you are feeding. Be realistic about the wedding cake size that you really need. A four or five tier wedding cake can be flashy, but most couples only need two or three tiers at most. If you want to add extra tiers, consider opting for artificial tiers. Styrofoam can be decorated to look like a real tier and will also cost less. You could also consider renting or buying a Styrofoam show-cake from a baker (many do this for larger functions) and have the caterer serve your guests from sheet cakes that are plated in a back kitchen.

Keeping the cake simple and avoiding fussy or handmade decorations will save you coin. If you **choose a basic cake style** instead of one with multiple flavours, icings, fillings, and decorations, the price will be reflective.

A cake is a cake right? Well first up, there is nothing stopping you from going to a local bakery and ordering decorated cakes to create your own-tiered ensemble. **Don't mention the word wedding**; ask for simple design or if you trust their skills and want a decorated cake, go for it. You can rent cake tiers from catering companies and bakeries for minimal cost or you can make your own.

Once your guests are tucking in, they won't know the difference (or care). There's nothing more elegant than a simple white cake topped with fresh flowers. **Fresh flowers** are a wonderful way to decorate cakes and a great way to tie your theme together. Whether you have a matching bouquet or the same colour scheme, fresh flowers look glamorous and are not hard to place on the cake yourself and look good. (Just check that they aren't toxic, or sprayed before putting them anywhere near the cake!)

> Well first up, there is nothing stopping you from going to a local bakery and ordering decorated cakes to create your own-tiered ensemble.

SWEETS

Look for a hobby baker or decorator, someone who has completed classes and is keen for experience. Professional cake makers, although often fabulously talented, have overheads such as rent and staffing costs that they work into the overall price. You can find some bargains by seeking out **home bakers** who still work out of their own kitchen. Shop around and get references. Do they deliver? Has their kitchen been inspected by health and safety? Have they worked in different temperatures (this is particularly important for summer events)? If you aren't completely sure of their skills, order a smaller test cake.

The **cupcake wedding cake/stand** is still massively popular and there are plenty of bakers now specialising in making and decorating cupcakes. Cupcakes are cute and neat all stacked up in a tiered style. Cupcake stands are also readily available on eBay and there is quite a good resale chance as well. Most cupcake wedding cakes feature a smaller cake on the top tier so the bride and groom still have a cake to cut.

The other main benefit of cupcake wedding cakes are that **guests can serve themselves.** One of the trickiest scams of the wedding business is the 'cake plating charge' or 'cakage'. It can range from $3 (£2) to $8 a slice just to 'plate the cake'. What a load of BS.

Instead of a grand tiered cake, why not create a **dessert bar** with pastries, smaller cakes, mousse, candy and biscuits. You can ask your bridal party and extended family to bring along their favourite dessert. A dessert table not only looks scrumptious it also gives your guests lots of options other than just a wedding cake. Again, with this one check with your venue to make sure they aren't going to lug you with extra costs.

You could replace the cake entirely with a chocolate fountain! **Chocolate fountains** are a very popular addition. Chocolate fountain rental companies will supply everything you need to have a delicious chocolate or caramel fountain flowing throughout your wedding reception. Usually fountains cost between $200 to $500 (£120-320) depending on the style you select and generally will include an operator to manage the fountain and clean-up.

smart STEPS

* The simpler the cake the cheaper it's going to be.

* If you want a four tiered cake but only need two tiers, use 'fake cakes', saving money and food.

* Create a dessert bar with lots of variety and yummy cakes and additions.

* Calculate the cost per head for each piece of cake, it's an easy way to bring you back to reality when considering a $2,000 (£1,200) cake.

SMART WEDDING   41

FLOWERS

We spent $250 (£160) on flowers for our wedding and no they weren't plastic and were not purchased from a supermarket or convenience store. We budgeted $300 (£190). We were stoked.

When choosing wedding flowers (if you want flowers at all) it's a smart idea to select **blooms that are in season** as they will be cheaper and, most importantly, available. Flowers such as gerberas, daisies, carnations and chrysanthemums, in comparison to roses and orchids, are usually very reasonably priced. Choose irises, violets, daffodils and tulips in spring. Lilies are plentiful and most affordable in the summer months. Roses and orchids are usually quite pricey despite the fact that they are widely available throughout the year. **Flower wholesalers** can save you over 50% of your wedding day flower costs for both your bouquets and table decorations.

Flower wholesalers cut out the middleman and sometimes you can even

From the earliest times, brides have adorned their hair with flowers and carried bunches of flowers. Traditionally, each type of flower had a special meaning and significance in and of itself. Flowers were often thrown at the couple after the ceremony. However today, most brides pick their flowers for colour and personal appeal not based on the traditional meaning of particular flowers.

visit the flower markets early in the morning (like the florists do!) to select the freshest and most beautiful flowers on the day! Many wholesalers won't arrange the flowers for you, so be advised to research some **flower arranging techniques,** watch some videos online and have a practice run before your wedding day. Basic bouquets are easy to make and they won't take too much time. You can buy flowers the day before and store them in the fridge overnight.

Ask the wholesaler for advice about removing any pollen buds, or snipping the heads off the stamen, because pollen can stain clothing as well as cause allergic reactions. When you are creating a floral arrangement, order plenty of greenery and 'spray' to increase flower volume in bouquets, they give the impression of more flowers. You might also pad out arrangements by including branches from your favourite flowering tree (Japanese blossoms look wonderful).

Local farmers' markets are an easy place to contact farmers and flower growers direct. Get there early and be prepared to travel to their farm or place of business to collect your order. Although this may seem inconvenient, you can save money and also get the freshest possible flowers available.

Big **supermarkets** and chains can mean big savings. Although there's nothing quaint about saying, "We got all of our flowers at Costco", there is something quite amazing about their packages. For example, one wedding collection advertised for $450 (£290) will get you:

20-piece Alstroemeria Wedding Collection

1 Bridal Bouquet
2 Bridesmaid Bouquets
3 Centrepieces (vases not included)
1 Toss Away Bouquet
1 Rose Petal Buds
4 Boutonnieres
4 Corsages
4 Wrist Corsages

Questions for Florists

- ☐ Is there a delivery or onsite set up fee?
- ☐ What time will they be arriving?
- ☐ If the flowers you choose aren't available on the day, does the florist pick the substitute or do you?
- ☐ Will they collect any rental items, vases etc post wedding?
- ☐ Do they have another wedding booked on the day of your wedding?

If you want to use a florist don't go to the trendiest place in town. Look for **smaller florists** a bit out of town and avoid well-known chains. Like any wedding business you can bargain with professional florists. And again compromise, if you want an elaborate bouquet cut out the floral centrepieces and church or reception floral decorations.

Take the time to see if their work is worth paying for and if in doubt ask the florist for some **references** and photographs of their work. Also, when buying from a florist eliminate the delivery fee by picking-up the flowers and decorations yourself or assigning a member of the wedding party to be in charge of this.

BOUQUETS, BOUTONNIÈRES AND CENTREPIECES

Flowers are here today, dead tomorrow. Granted, they look pretty and smell nice but they don't need to be everywhere, being clutched by everyone. Before you get angry at me for killing your floral fun, I'm not suggesting you cut flowers completely, just make the ones you do use count.

Larger blooms will often get you more bang for your buck. Think hydrangeas, lilies, rhododendrons and peonies, they're big, bold, take up more room and cut down

It's a smart idea to select blooms that are in season as they will be cheaper and, most importantly, available.

on cost. Also, consider using filler leaves, ferns, hydrangea leaves, limoniums and solidagos to add volume and complement floral arrangements.

Bridesmaids don't necessarily need individual bouquets, instead of giving bridesmaids costly bouquets to lug around, pin **one beautiful blossom** on each of your attendants; a lady boutonnière or even an old school but gorgeous wrist corsage. A much more inexpensive option and this way the flowers have become part of their outfit and not left on a table in the bathrooms after an hour.

For groomsmen **boutonnières** look fabulous and if they aren't wearing matching suits or outfits, this small detail can really tie them together.

You don't need a massive floral centrepiece to make the table gorgeous. In fact you don't need flowers on the table at all. Using floral arrangements on each table is hugely expensive and perhaps a tad wasteful, especially if you're having a large wedding.

If you are really keen on having some sort of **'living' centrepiece** but can't afford a full floral arrangement then visit your local garden centre or nursery and buy several trays of annuals or perennials that match your colour scheme. You could also choose herbs, like oregano, basil, and tarragon, which will give any setting an organic feel; and I'll guarantee they will be whipped up by the guests to take home at the end of the day.

SMART WEDDING 45

Instead of elaborate floral centrepieces that are filled with blooms (that in my opinion hinder guests from seeing anything on the other side of the table), consider using petite vases or **vintage jars** and fill them with a few flower stems. We chose yellow tulips for our wedding, which were compact, colourful and neat. We purchased 5 bunches from the florist for $15 (£9.50) each and asked the florist ahead of time as to when the flowers would bloom. This worked perfectly because we picked our flowers up the day before the wedding and they matured and bloomed overnight.

Ripe fruits are said to symbolise abundance and fertility … they're also yummy, cheap and colourful. Tomatoes look beautiful and enticing in a rustic Italian display. You could include green or red apples, peaches, vibrant lemons or limes, grapes or pomegranates; stack them in cases, spray paint them, stick name cards in them, experiment away.

Candles create an air of romanticism and can be bought in all shapes and sizes. Gather different sized candles together on vintage plates or trays. Sit them in vases surrounded by pebbles. You can buy the pebbles and pillar candles from dollar shops, Target and Kmart. While you are looking at these discount shops you can also look for hurricane vases and plain pillar vases, which also look great with candles placed inside (especially if your venue will not allow open flames without a cover, which is most venues). Pet stores and nurseries sell pebbles in a variety of colours and textures (for fish tanks and fountains).

smart STEPS

- Use local vendors.
- Use alternative decorations for table centrepieces and ceremony decorations.
- Use in season flowers.
- Choose simple arrangements that you can create yourself.
- Visit flower markets and wholesalers. Negotiate, negotiate, negotiate.

Let's get busy: DECORATIONS

If you are hiring a gallery or a standard function centre or hotel, it's nice to add a personalised touch with decorations, tableware and flowers. Indoor locations, like museums and vineyards may need less adornment, but it's not hard or expensive to decorate. You don't have to be Martha Stewart or a pro with a sewing machine (although basic hand sewing skills can help) to give your wedding a touch of you.

SMART WEDDING

Before you go out and buy anything, speak to your venue manager or coordinator to see if they have any decorations, such as candles, lanterns, vases or lights that you could use for free or hire at a small cost. It's **better to borrow** than buy.

Decorative items do not have to be purchased from a homewares shop; in fact it's best to avoid them all together. You are going to make what they sell. All of our best buys came from places you wouldn't expect, like hardware stores, post offices and discount emporiums.

When looking for decorative items, **pick versatile materials,** things that you can use for a number of wedding related projects. Recycle when you can and change the way you look at household items… they can be transformed into the star of the show with a little bit of DIY magic.

Hessian

Hessian (burlap) is a versatile wedding decoration resource and it's **CHEAP**. It's durable and reliable and not only is it a great budget back up material, it's also one of the world's most environmentally friendly fibres, 100% biodegradable and it's grown quickly without pesticide and chemicals. It looks **rustic** cut into triangles as bunting, bound around decorative jars or bouquets, and as table runners. If your ceremony location has uneven ground, is rough or the grass is patchy, using hessian as an aisle runner is a quick fix (use tent pegs to secure it). All items can be purchased at the hardware store. Hessian usually retails at under $6 (£4) per metre.

Sew it baby

If tablecloths are supplied for free with the venue, they will generally be white. You can jazz up a bland venue with the **addition of colour** and movement, such as a patterned table runner or colourful napkins, which can easily be sewn at home with even the most basic sewing skills. Using contrasting napkins in your theme can be quite striking against the white of the tablecloth. Scour second hand shops, eBay and Etsy for vintage material to use as tablecloths or runners. A floral or vintage bohemian theme can be pretty without being overly pink or feminine.

Bed sheets from Target, Walmart, Kmart and IKEA are often inexpensive (and cheaper than material by the foot or metre) and can be used as tablecloths or cut into strips for table runners or napkins. Table runners can be bold or blend into the linen, carrying your colour theme(s) through the venue to make a statement.

Our caterer was happy to supply linen at a cost ... a cost that I found reasonably exorbitant ($35 (£22) per tablecloth for hire). After some research I found a company on eBay that was a hospitality industry wholesaler that sold direct to the public. I purchased 12 tablecloths for $11 (£8) each. They were **heavy duty** and fairly **stain resistant**, so much so, post wedding I was able to home launder them and resell on eBay for the same price to another bride. Suck it caterers.

How to Sew a Napkin (Easy peasy)

Sewing cloth napkins is a great way to practice your sewing machine skills with the whole project essentially just being able to sew four hemmed sides on a piece of fabric. It's basic and because they are 'handmade' you can get away with them looking a little rustic and au naturel. I sewed 60 napkins over Easter weekend. It was a great goal and they looked fabulous if I do say so myself.

A luncheon napkin is usually 12" square, whereas a dinner napkin can be anywhere from 18" to 20" square. If you are sewing (possibly over 100 napkins) I suggest going for the smaller sized napkins.

What you need:
Fabric
Thread
Scissors
Ruler
Iron and ironing board
A sewing machine (or if you prefer to hand sew, patience)

1. Cut fabric into squares about 1½ inches larger than desired finished size, i.e. for a 12-inch square napkin, cut a 13½ inch square of fabric.
2. Iron under all edges ¼ inch.
3. Using the pressing lines as a guide, iron the corner triangle down or for a neater, less bulky edge, trim off a triangle from each corner.
4. Pin the ironed hemline in place.
5. With folded sides facing down, stitch very close to the inner edge of the hem on one side, stopping at each corner, with the machine needle in the down position, and turn the napkin 90° and stitch the next side.
6. Tie off thread ends.

SMART WEDDING

CUT THE FAT AND THE FROOF

In my opinion, chair sashes and covers are over… and they are the item that I would first lose if you were looking to save money. A lot of function centres insist on you hiring them because they supply god-awful, plastic chairs that are both an eye sore and an arse sore.

Chair covers are not to everyone's taste and quite frankly a big pink satin bow or lycra style, elasticised seat cover, well, I think they're froofy and ugly, but hey, no judgment, if you think spending $9 (£6) on a chair cover is worth the money then go for it!

A neat **folding wooden chair** (natural wood, black or white) looks far less fussy and is cheaper to hire. They can be personalised with a band of vintage material or small buntings and they come with a cushion. If bows are your thing, spend on, but otherwise ditch them.

In addition to the dining tables, you may want to decorate other extra tables such as the **cake table, guestbook** (if you are having one) and **gift table**. You could try using the same tablecloths and motifs as the main reception area … if in doubt tone it down and use a plain white tablecloth.

REUSE, RECYCLE AND GET CREATIVE

When you next finish a bottle of pasta sauce or condiments, **don't throw the jar away** … they're full of creative potential as unique wedding decorations. They can look chic and simple and can be used in SO many ways at a wedding as centrepieces, holding candles, fruit or bunches of flowers. Tall Passata jars (tomato sauce) are great for bouquets.

Until you start collecting them you probably won't realise just how many jars we

Cocktail jars

Smaller jars can be used for **cocktail hour.** Try matching them with decorative paper straws. They don't all have to match, in fact the more variety, the better they look.

Dessert Jars

Jars are the perfect serving size for **desserts** like cream and berries, yoghurt parfait or lava cakes. Make sure you clean the jars really well by soaking them in boiling water. Remember to keep hold of the lids and you can then attach a fork or a spoon with some twine. These also make a great take-home treat or bonbonniere.

Grow your own bonbonniere

A very simple bonbonniere project is to gift your guests **a plant or seedling**. Using your collection of recycled jars, fill them with soil and compost, sprinkle some seeds inside, place on a windowsill and water whenever the soil is dry. Allow the flowers or plants plenty of time to grow! Keep the flowers + dirt in the jars and use as terrarium-style centrepieces or live-bouquets.

Live plants bring a natural element to both indoor and outdoor weddings. It's also a wonderful way to save money, considering that a pack of 50 seeds is about $3 (£1.90).

Paint 'em

Glass Jars don't have to stay clear. Using glass paint you can create an opaque effect or spray paint will create more of a solid

go through and all of the different shapes and patterns that are available. It took my husband and I eight months to collect about 200 jars and bottles. We put out facebook messages and emails to friends and family, asking them not to throw their jars away.

Once you collect the jars, they're going to need a soak and scrub before they're ready to appear in your wedding. We put them through the dishwasher and then used eucalyptus oil to clean off any stubborn labels.

colour. If there are patterns or lettering on the glass it will give an embossed effect, fabulous for a vintage/shabby-chic wedding.

Lights

LED bulbs or white Christmas lights are a fun and easy way to create that starry night, romantic atmosphere. Weaving them through trees outside, around ugly pillars or creating a **night sky effect** inside on the ceiling is easy (you just don't want to be the one taking them down later!). If you plan ahead you can hit the post Christmas sales where Christmas tree lights are often in the bargain bin.

Literary additions

Do you like to read? Or perhaps even just pretend to like to read? Then make books a part of your wedding décor. It's hip and smart and they are everywhere. Buy a bunch of old (non collectable) **vintage books** from a charity or second hand shop, and stack them as centrepieces on each table.

Use a book as a table number (print a new cover or use a stick on number) or if you're really clever (and have mad graphic design skills, or know someone who does) use your favourite books as a theme, naming each table after them. Work your names into the book title or if you're particularly vain or showy, have the book cover re-jigged to include you.

Scrabble tiles are from hipster wedding heaven. You can buy bags of mismatched, board-less tiles on eBay and use them all over reception venue, stick them everywhere! Again they can spell out guest's names, table numbers, seating charts. You can also create jewellery and cufflinks from the tiles, using pre-bought accessories and superglue.

Typewriters are also funky as hell. You can grab a second-hand typewriter online or from local bazaars, charity shops and markets. Replace the ribbon (which you can score online) and you're on your way. Have your guests type out their messages for you. Whip out your favourite literary quotes (probably about marriage, sex, love, weddings etc...), and use them on the back of guest cards. It can be a conversation topic for guests or just add a touch of poetic romance and instant faux intelligence.

Old fashion **library checkout cards** make gorgeous place-name settings and literary confetti* made from book pages is

> Check with your venue if they allow confetti as some venues and churches have banned it ...yes banned.

52 SMART WEDDING

always a hit! There are a number of online retailers that specialise in paper confetti hearts, lovingly up-cycled from old Mills and Boon romance novels. Kooky, fun AND recycled, you couldn't ask for more.

*Check with your venue if they allow confetti as some venues and churches have banned it … yes banned. Killjoys. I mean, really.

Paper lanterns and pom poms

Paper lanterns add colour (and light) to a reception venue. If the ceiling's disagreeable or boring, **stringing up some lanterns** is a bold and low cost solution. They are light and can be hung on fishing line, so no damage to walls and ceilings. Lanterns are produced in every colour under the sun and you can even choose to have battery-operated lamps inside the lanterns to give them a beautiful glow. They don't scream 'Asian wedding', of course if that's what you're after, there are plenty with symbols and images attached. Bulk bargains can be found online but if you live in a city, head straight to an Asian emporium, supermarket or Chinatown.

Remember they are paper, not waterproof and can look pretty sad when wet, so if there is a possibility of rain, hold off putting them up until the last possible minute (they are also not colourfast when wet … lesson learned).

If you are feeling crafty, and let's face it, who isn't? **Tissue paper pom poms** can easily be made at home and doing this will save you a bomb. What's great about these pom poms is that you can buy tissue paper (again from discount and haberdashery shops) very cheaply and you can colour match.

DIY POM POMS

What you need:
Tissue paper (10 sheets per pom)
Thin wire (you can use florist wire or fine electrical wire from the hardware store)
Scissors
Fishing line for hanging

1. Stack 10 sheets of tissue paper.

2. Make 1½ inch wide accordion folds, creasing with your fingers with each fold.

3. Fold a 15-17 inch piece of wire in half, and slip over the centre of the folded tissue; twist and secure. To save fiddling when the pom is in full splendour, tie a length of fishing line to the wire for hanging.

4. Round the edge of the tissue with scissors (or cut any pattern you like).

5. Separate layers, pulling away from the centre one at a time.

Hey presto a fancy pom pom!
   If you want to mix things up you can alternate the colours of the tissue paper to create a rainbow or multi-coloured effect.

smart
STEPS

✸ If you are going to get your DIY on, do it with plenty of time. You don't want to be sewing napkins the night before the wedding.

✸ Choose projects that are worth your time. Don't hand paint 480 jars if A, you could buy them cheaper and B, no one is going to notice your handy work.

✸ Utilise places like craft shops, discount suppliers and IKEA.

✸ Themes can be subtle, you don't need to knock your guests over the head with it.

✸ Use Grandmas, mother in laws and crafty friends to help you out. If they're keen to help out, give small talks and jobs.

Wedding magazines
AT 15 BUCKS A POP, are they worth it?

No, of course not. You have this book. Next chapter.

Wedding
MAGAZINES

I kid … well sort of.
In the excitement, as soon as they get engaged, most brides are quick off the mark to pop down to the newsagency and spend about $50 (£30) on 3 bridal magazines.

There is no doubt they are lovely looking publications, with lots of glamorous photographs and filled with ads for vendors, but the cheapest magazine is generally around $15.95 (£10), which is the equivalent of buying a book … a book filled with advertisements.

Most capital cities and some regional areas have their own wedding publication. This is often the **best value magazine** as they have a list of local vendors and often their own website, so you have an immediate resource for vendors, all in one document. eBay is also the place to score bulk wedding magazines as brides offload their used magazines, so make sure if you do purchase new magazines to keep them in good condition as they are an easy resell.

BUYING AN ENGAGEMENT RING AND WEDDING BAND; HOW TO SPOT A GOOD DIAMOND

Look, by now you probably have a ring on it but if you don't or are looking for more **diamonds** for your wedding band (stop it!) then it is important to know what you are buying. There are a lot of dodgy dealers out there who will charge big dollars for crap diamonds.

Have you seen the film *Blood Diamond*? Go away and watch it now. Yes you will feel bad and guilty but in exchange you would have spent over an hour with Leonardo DiCaprio, so get over it.

It's not just African warlords and smugglers that rain on the engagement ring parade. My Grandmother's best friend wore her engagement ring for 45 years and only found out that her diamond was a fake when the setting needed adjusting and the stone began to melt when the jeweller applied heat to it.

She was devo.

Don't let this happen to you.

Understand the four Cs

Carat
Colour
Clarity
Cut

The quality and value of a diamond is judged on four fundamental criteria known as the four Cs. The carat-weight, colour, clarity and cut. Some differences in quality are easily noticeable, others need specialist equipment and qualified graders with years of experience to assess and detect. **Accurate assessment** of a diamond is only possible prior to being set. Once the stone is set even a trained grader cannot precisely determine colour, size and purity. Therefore quality and value can only be estimated. Minor differences in colour, clarity and weight can have a major effect on the value. For this reason, laboratories only grade loose diamonds.

Carat

Weight is the most obvious factor in determining the value of a diamond. But two diamonds of equal weight can have very unequal values, depending on their quality. Furthermore, **weight** only indicates size, and depending on proportions two diamonds weighing the same may appear very different in size.

Colour

Most gem quality diamonds fall within a range from **"D" colourless** to **"Z" light yellow.**

Almost all have a trace of yellow, brown or grey body colour. The differences between colours are very subtle and graded according to the International Colour Grading Scale. With the exception of some natural fancy colours, such as blue, pink, purple, yellow or red, the colourless grade is the most valuable.

Clarity

Diamonds may have various **inclusions** or **imperfections**. The number and size of these determines the clarity grading. Most imperfections in gem quality diamonds are not visible to the naked eye. For this reason clarity is graded under 10-x magnification.

Cut

The cut of a diamond is the only property which is totally dependent on man. Cut refers not only to the **shape and style** of the diamond, but its **proportions, symmetry, and finish** or **"make"**. Proportions and angles influence the internal reflection of light as well as the dispersion of light leaving the diamond.

This determines the brilliance and fire (brightness and sparkle) of the diamond, and ultimately its perceived beauty. Cut, therefore, is actually one of the most important aspects to consider when choosing your diamond. A diamond can be cut for maximum weight recovery or maximum brilliance and beauty. Invariably one is traded off at the expense of the other. Although poor makes sell at a discount in the trade, realistically the unsuspecting retail customer will pay the same price regardless of make. Ultimately **taste** and **preference** for the overall appearance determine the buyer's choice.

smart STEPS

✱ Make sure the diamond and ring come with adequate certification.

✱ If you are buying online make sure to do your research … really do your research.

✱ Look for up-and-coming jewellers.

✱ Bigger is not always better, especially when it comes to the quality of the stone.

Don't wear that

The bridal gown/dress/suit for most brides is an essential part of the day. Finding your outfit could take weeks, months or even years. It's a big decision. Do you want to be a meringue? A bedazzled beauty? An Annie Hall or a fifties starlet? Before you cross the threshold of any bridal shop, have a wee baby think about what YOU want to wear and who (if anyone) you want there to help you decide.

Wedding dress shopping is an **emotive** and **fun** process (for most) but it can also be stressful and overwhelming. If you ever watched *Say yes to the dress* or any of the similar wedding reality TV shows, you know that most of the drama centres on over-opinionated a-hole friends and family, whose main goal it seems is to upset the bride and make her feel bad about her body/dress choices. Of course TV shows are contrived but they do highlight the importance of only taking along someone whose opinion you trust and who knows when to talk up and when to shut up.

Before hitting the shops with 16 of your closest friends and family, why not take yourself out for a **solo shopping trip**? You don't have to try anything on, just peruse … pick a couple of shops that you would like to return to with your designated helper(s) and take some time to formulate a dress plan.

You might already have a clear picture of what you want to look and feel like, including the shape, the colour and theme. Or, like a majority of brides, you may be clueless and have no idea what you are going to wear and can't picture your head on *any* of the dresses in bridal magazines. That's cool … I mean how many of us have worn a silk/satin evening gown on a regular basis and know what suits them and what looks god-awful? Princesses we are not.

When it comes to wedding dress styles the options are close to endless and when looking for your dress think outside the box … don't just look at bridal shops. Department stores and high street retailers not only stock white and cream dresses and ensembles, many have caught on to the idea of releasing a limited edition bridal range. Why not a look at designer frocks? You can buy a Chanel suit for the same price as an average wedding gown AND you could wear it again AND you can say "Hey I own a Chanel Suit!"

When choosing an outfit, whether you are going to buy from a bridal shop or not, it is a good idea to visit a boutique where you can try on a number of dresses to find a style that suits you. It's one thing to pick something out of a magazine; it's another to see what it **looks like on you**. We're all different shapes, heights and sizes. You know what you like, which body parts you're happy to show off and what you'd rather ensconce in form fitting fabric. I'm going to be brutal here so get ready.

> When looking for your dress think outside the box … don't just look at bridal shops.

I have a confession. I purchased a traditional strapless dress. I was totally sucked in. It was pretty but every time I tried it on, I kept hitching it up, something wasn't right. I didn't get that 'you look totes amaze' feeling when I tried it on. When I visualised our wedding day I couldn't see me in that dress. It was like someone had smuggled me out of my own imagination!

We were getting married in the depths of winter and I was worried about being cold (yes I realise I sound like an octogenarian).

I wanted the dress to look 'different' so I thought, let's add a belt! Fourteen belts later. No go. How about a bolero? A sash? A funky cardigan? A wrap? A sequined throw? Waaaaaaaaaaaaa.

How about … *this dress is all wrong and I totally fell for the bridal industry BS about what I am supposed to look like*?

Yep.

A month before our wedding I called my best friend and said "I'm embarrassed to say this but the dress isn't right and I wonder if you have a couple of hours to go shopping?"

She was at my house within the hour. We went on a fast and furious shopping binge, visiting a big department store and picking every cream and white dress that we could find off the racks. Our venue was a 50s house … it was stylised. I love the *Mad Men*-just getting married at the Town Hall or registry office look!

Why, why, why did I buy that big froofy dress that ate me?

With every little vintage style shift dress that I tried on, I realised that the dress I had was all wrong. By three that afternoon I had chosen a gorgeous cream Marino wool Jersey dress that not only made me feel amazing, it covered the bits that I wanted to cover and showed off the bits that I have worked really hard for! I loved it. It was $300 (£190) and I couldn't have been happier.

Strapless gowns can look pretty bad on most people.

Really bad.

Ok?

Sorry.

I know they are on trend and every Jane and Jill buys them but if you've got a larger rack, bingo wings, a tummy, you're short, you're super skinny … well look, they're hard to pull off and really, to be honest, they can look pretty mediocre.

My point is; YOU wear what makes YOU feel gorgeous and comfortable on your wedding day. It's YOUR day to shine. Not what a magazine tells you to wear. YOU want to look and feel like a jazzed up version of you. Not a character. YOU want to look back on these photographs and think *Gee whiz, I looked smashing*, not, *Why in the hell are my boobs hanging out?*

If your arms aren't as toned as you'd like then cover them up; get a pashmina, a dress with a cap sleeve, a bolero, or a jacket. If you're flat chested, don't wear ridiculous chicken fillet boob cups, that's not you and to be honest it would probably just look weird. Are you normally pale? Well then perhaps don't go for the ultra mahogany tan. Again, you'll look weird and guests will spend more time talking about the tan rubbing off on your beautiful dress than how in love you guys are and what a beautiful couple you make.

Bridal boutiques are good for **advice**. Use them, even if you have no intention of not purchasing a gown from a boutique. Every bride should go and try on something truly overpriced and ridiculously froofy. It's part of the wedding planning experience. It's also a great way to figure out what you don't like, which is often more helpful than knowing what you do like. This way you can eliminate styles and cuts that don't make you hum.

When trying on a dress firstly ask – **is it comfortable?** You want to look and feel great. You don't want to be hitching it up, worried it's going fall down etc. If you want to dance on the day, don't buy a dress where bending isn't a possibility. Think about what sort of dress is most appropriate for your day. A heavily corseted bodice might not be appropriate if you intend to sit or eat at the reception. Also a hooped skirt will probably not suit a beach wedding. Bridal boutiques in no way expect a sale out of every customer and often welcome multiple visits if you can't decide.

Wedding dresses are mostly hugely expensive rip offs and brides, upon finding ***the dress***, can quickly disregard budget, lose their heads and end up paying more for a gown that they will wear for six hours than a small car. Like any major purchase in life, shop around, take your time and do not be pressured. Even if you love the dress, go away and think it over. Don't succumb to the pressure of sales assistants. They know how to make a sale, especially the ones on commission (sorry ladies).

Wedding dress sales tactics

Panic!
"Oh, you have 6 months before your wedding? REALLY? Oh dear, you'd better make your mind up quick or you won't be able to get any dress!"

Rubbish. Yes, some manufactures require 6 months to order a dress, have it made and get it to the bride but there are plenty of off the rack, take home and get married tomorrow options.

Repetition
Sales assistants repeat back what you have asked for. "That really is a stunning organza gown with fish tail pleats ... it's just what you asked for."

Ok robot.

Lies
"If you come back this dress might not be available is a month/week/hour."

This goes against the basic fundamentals of capitalism. They are lying to you.

The Fancy Fabrics fibs
Traditional wedding dresses come in silk or artificial fibres. Satin, crepe organza, taffeta and chiffon refer to the way the fibre has been manufactured and woven. Both silk and artificial fibres can be woven into satin, organza etc. Silk is expensive and most certainly is used as an up-selling point by sales people. "Feel the quality", etc. Many synthetic fabrics look and feel just as nice as silk and are a quarter of the cost. Check the label and if 'genuine silk' isn't mentioned, assume it is synthetic.

No Tag?
Bridal shops often re-tag gowns, meaning they remove original information and replace it with their own. This is often done to prevent you from comparison-shopping. If this is the case ask for the correct style number and designer information. Be honest and tell them you are doing your research. A reputable business realises that people shop around and will work hard to make sure you buy from them.

Don't reveal your budget, in fact get them to show you gowns that are under budget as sales assistants tend to throw in a couple of "this is a little (usually $1,000+ (£630+)) over your budget but I just **HAD** to show you". This is bad and manipulative and a bit bitchy. By underselling your limits, they'll more than likely bring you dresses that are on par with your limits.

Remember in no way are the prices inflexible. Wedding gown trends move quickly. You can score a bargain by purchasing a 'last season' dress. Many stores discount heavily to shift stock. They might not disclose that fact directly but by asking for their 'best price' you can often receive a sizable discount.

If you find the dress that you want to buy then firstly ... well done ... secondly, be cool.

Trust me, unless it's a one of a kind, only dress in the world ... they **CAN** order more, even if they try and sell you an excuse about it being 'limited edition'... yeah one of only 8,000. Just like wedding reception venues, wedding sales assistants have a healthy collection of tactics they use to convince you to **PAY NOW**.

Bridal gown designers and manufacturers generally deal exclusively with one bridal shop in an area; so if you want to get a good idea of the selection available, visit a number of shops. If you are keen to purchase from a bridal salon always enter with a bargaining attitude.

Ask:
"Will you discount for cash payments?"
"What is the final price and what does the price include?"
"Does the price include alterations?"

Get them to provide you with this in writing, particularly if you require complicated alterations ... you don't want to get stung with another bill!
"Will you sell store samples or floor stock?"

With the change of seasons, bridal boutiques often sell their sample gowns to smart brides and second hand designer clothing shops. If the boutique won't sell you the sample direct, by doing a bit of research and contacting nearby **second-hand** retailers, it's often possible to get a heads up when new stock is received from the boutique (bridal boutiques often don't like this information to be made public). Although you may think a second hand sample gown is not for you, think again. After dry cleaning (which you can also try and negotiate through the shop) some dresses *can* be like new. After all, many bridal shop dresses are looked after extremely well; they are maintained and cared for because they are what make the sale.

The dresses are usually **sample sizes** (and sometimes rather random sizes) that the shop was unable to sell or lines that they are no longer stocking. As always use caution and inspect the dress thoroughly before purchasing. If beading is missing, ask if the store can help you replace them. Check for make up stains and try the dress on to make sure it is true to size. Remember it's only a bargain if you don't have to spend hundreds of dollars repairing and resizing it.

CLICKITY CLACK TIPPITY TAP, FINDING DRESS LOVE ONLINE

The online wedding industry is booming and with exchange rates between the **UK, USA** and **Australia** reasonably favourable you can find bargains.

Designer and **name-brand gowns** that are found in boutiques can usually be purchased online at a much cheaper rate. If you find a dress you love in store, record as much information as possible, names, item numbers etc. Try it on and get the correct sizing.

Some overseas suppliers and stores will ship directly to you, therefore cutting out the middleman and commissions. If you are going down this road, then remember to be careful. If it sounds too good to be true then it probably is.

Online

www.netbride.com (US)
www.davidsbridal.com/index.jsp (US)
www.bargainweddinggowns.com/ (US)
www.shopshop.com/ (US)
www.rsvpbridal.com/ (US)
www.ultimatebridewire.com/ (US)
www.ebay.com
www.etsy.com
www.foreverbrides.com/ (US)

Online sellers have lower pricing due to the high volume of sales they are able to achieve and lower overheads. You just need to use the same caution in choosing what online company to deal with as you would with selecting a bridal shop. If they seem dodgy, then bail. Most of the badmouthing and gossip mongering about the online bridal wear industry comes from bridal shops themselves. They're losing out, so of course they'd hate it. They will warn you of fake and defective gowns, which you'll find in bridal boutiques too. If you research, read forums and talk to other buyers then savings will be had.

Factor in to the cost any importation or **duty taxes** that may be added to items. This can be up to 20% in some countries. Does the supplier have refund, exchange and return options available? Ask questions to ensure that they will take the gown back if it arrives with a flaw and replace it immediately at no cost to you. (They should also pay all postage associated with the return.) Have a seamstress take your measurements and if in doubt order a size up, as it is a lot easier to take a dress in than come up with creative ways to make it bigger.

Bridal shops (in nearly all cases) will not accept exchanges. The gowns are ordered just for you from the manufacturer. If you place a deposit at a shop it is non-refundable. It is best to be sure of your gown, price and additional details before placing a deposit.

PRE-SALE - RE-SALE

Think about the possible re-sale price when buying items for your wedding. There are loads of smart brides out there, just like you, who are selling and buying their wedding day items online. Hey, they've only been used for a day! Get amongst it. **Consigning** and **selling wedding gowns** and accessories is a clever move for brides both in store and online.

Something that is very popular is selling the gown before the bride has even walked down the aisle.

Bridal shops (in nearly all cases) will not accept exchanges. If you place a deposit at a shop it is non-refundable. It is best to be sure of your gown, price and additional details before placing a deposit.

Ah ha. Yep. Prior to wearing the dress, it's already sold. Pre-sale. Securing the next wearer of the dress before you've worn it. It's a great idea and a way to wear a possibly very expensive gown at a fraction of the cost. It's sort of like hiring.

Seeing the value and embracing this idea for some brides may require a change of perspective, instead of seeing the dress as something you pay $8,000 (£5,000) for and keep for your daughter to wear (by the way I'm 99% sure she is NOT going to wear the dress… **would YOU wear your mother's dress?** Seriously? This tradition is pushy and over-romanticised).

Anyway, instead of seeing it as something that you will keep forever, think of the dress as a commodity. If you buy a popular design, perhaps a Vera Wang gown for $4,500 (£2,800), you can advertise the same gown for $3,800 (£2,420), before you've worn it. After the wedding day, the dress is dry-cleaned, packed (dry cleaner will do this for you at a cost) and then shipped to its next owner. As long as you look after the dress, this is a super way to wear a **$4,500** (£2,800), **gown for $1,000** (£650).

If you do enter an agreement with another bride, as always be honest, clear and open in your communication. Let them know exactly what you are providing. If you live close by, meet up and view the dress in advance. Use an escrow service or PayPal if you are worried about any transactional issues.

If your seamstress knows you'll be selling your dress, they can leave additional fabric in the seams (undetectable to you,

Second time's a charm

www.oncewed.com
www.preownedweddingdresses.com
www.woreitonce.com
www.recycledbride.com
www.thebrideslist.com
www.usedweddingdresses.com
www.indiebride.com

SMART WEDDING

but helpful to the next bride), or they can save the extra fabric so you can pass it along for future alterations.

Of course you can't predict the future; you don't know what's going to happen on your wedding day. You could spill something, rip a hem or sit on a cake, so if that occurs talk to the buyer (or seller) beforehand about who is liable for any incurred repairs, and if the dress is written off completely then make sure you create a contract that will allow you to bail on the agreement.

Lastly, if you are the buyer, ask if the dress has been altered. If you're 6'2" and the original owner is 5'1", then I'm guessing you are going to have some issues.

If **pre-selling** is something you are keen on, **plan ahead**, don't alter the garment drastically and don't be greedy. Listing the dress at full price will get you nowhere. If done properly this is a fabulous way to get a smashing dress for less, not waste a gorgeous gown (sitting in the cupboard for 10 years) and pay its wonderfulness forward.

Here are some tips for selling your dress online:

FAB PICTURES: Clear pictures of your dress will help tell its story. Show the front, back and details of the dress on a person so buyers can see how it fits. (A perfect excuse to show off some of your beautiful wedding pictures!) If you don't want to show your face, smudge it out in Photoshop.

DESCRIPTION: Provide details on your dress as if buyers are unfamiliar with it. Describe the fabric, the fit, the details and any alterations you made. The more information you can provide, the faster you will capture interest and make a sale.

PRICE: Reasonably priced dresses sell faster. A used wedding dress in good condition and less than three years old should be priced at 50% off retail.

LESS IS MORE

The simpler the wedding gown, the **less expensive** it is going to be. If you leave off the beading or embroidery, or simply switch the fabric of the gown you are going to save money.

Traditionally wedding dresses have not always been white. The popularity of the white and ivory wedding dress can be traced back to 1840 with the marriage of Queen Victoria to Albert of Saxe-Coburg. The Queen chose to wear a white gown for the event and the official wedding portrait photograph was widely published and many brides opted for a similar dress in honour of that choice. The tradition continues today. **Wedding dresses vary** right across the globe. Many wedding dresses in China are coloured red, the traditional colour of good luck. For brides in the northern parts of India the traditional colour of women's wedding garments is also red, a colour symbolising auspiciousness. The colour green is also commonly used, signifying fertility.

OK, so maybe red and green are a bit too full on for you but think laterally. You like the Betty Draper look? Then perhaps vintage is worth considering. With the popularity of *Mad Men*, **vintage dresses** (new and genuine) are massive with brides, especially with the classic 50s look of wider skirts and smaller accentuated waists. They're very flattering, chic, feminine and fabulous, accentuating an hourglass figure. Not only can you score an original and classic designer gem, you can guarantee that you won't see other brides swanning around in YOUR dress. If you don't want

---

Going old-school

www.thevintageweddingdresscompany.com
www.vintageous.com
www.poshgirlvintage.com
www.thefrock.com

SMART WEDDING

to buy online, hit vintage bazaars, fairs and second hand stores. Auction houses and deceased estates (grim I know but all classy dames eventually cark it and their gorgeous vintage wardrobes are out there for the taking) can also be fab.

There are hundreds (if not thousands) of specialty vintage dress vendors online. The disadvantage of buying vintage without trying on first is **sizing**. Sizes have changed, so be sure to ask for exact measurements. Look for general **wear and tear.** Ask where and how the dress has been stored. Are there visible mildew marks or stains? Moth holes? Has the dress been dry-cleaned? (This could actually be bad if the dress is really old, as some were not made for such a process). Is the colour exactly like the photograph (you would be surprised how different some of these dresses look to the photographs).

Wearing vintage is pretty special and the quality of formal dresses was usually of a very high standard.

REPLICA DRESSES

OK, this is a risk. I'm going to be honest. **A LOT** of replica dresses are substandard. BUT if you have your eye on an ultra expensive designer dress and cannot warrant paying the price, you may consider a 'designer inspired dress' or a replica or a rip-off.

The longest wedding dress train was found in Germany, it measured over 515 feet.

There are many thousands of companies that will replicate a gown from a photograph or sample for very little money. I'm talking $200-$500 (£130-320).

Before I go on I have to say quietly (and I am not guilt tripping, really I am not) that we should assume that most of these dresses are made in quasi-sweatshop style factories. Maybe not by kiddies but probably by people that should be paid more (actually even some authentic full prices dresses are made in these factories). No judgment, but I think you should ask questions about what you buy and where it comes from AND if you only pay $199 (£127) for a dress and bitch about its quality compared to the $7,000 (£4500) dress you tried on in the store, then you're going to need to suck it up. Also replicating designs is **against copyright laws** and counterfeit goods are illegal and can be impounded by customs, so be warned and beware. Saying all of that, you can get good results, with some brides saying that they couldn't even notice the difference from the designer gown. Aren't they lucky?

Most gowns that are ordered through these companies are produced and shipped from China or Eastern Europe. The online 'shop front' generally trades from the USA.

You know how I keep banging on about doing your research? Well, here it is again … do your research. There are forums devoted to brides that order from these companies. Brides post pictures of the dress that they ordered and then a photo of what they received. It is so helpful to see and read their genuine feedback to really get an idea of what you might be up for.

Many companies also allow customers' to post images of the dresses they receive, so you can see other customer's results. If you are going to try this avenue, give yourself decent lead-time. It often takes up to 6 weeks for the dress to be made and shipped and if there are any problems or alterations that need to be made to the gown, it will allow time for that to happen. Be as accurate as possible with descriptions and measurements. Most companies send you a measurement table for you to fill out. It is suggested that you visit a tailor or dressmaker to have your measurements accurately recorded. It is also better to be on the safer side, sizing the gown slightly larger, in case alterations are needed and therefore providing you with a seam allowance (it's better to spend the extra money having the gown altered than not being able to squeeze into it at all).

Companies will nearly always be happy to oblige you with material swatches and samples so you can be sure that the material is the quality and colour that you desire. Ordering the gown without sighting swatches isn't recommend as there are many definitions of the colour 'white' and 'ivory' (especially when different languages are involved!).

Some of these overseas manufacturers can be clever when combining features of different dresses. If you like the bodice of one dress, with the train of another and embroidery of another you can ask them to attempt to combine styles.

Do your homework and be ready to have the gown altered at home if you aren't happy with what arrives in the post.

DRESS STYLES

A-line

A-line dresses lengthen the whole body without drawing attention to your waistline. A-line wedding dresses are also flattering on petite women. This style is very simple and elegant. The A-line can be slender and narrow or it can be quite wide, requiring a hoop. You do need to bear in mind, however, the larger your hips, the wider the base of the skirt will be.

SMART WEDDING

Remember, you want to create an illusion of being tall and slim. If the skirt is too narrow, and your hips too wide, it will simply draw unnecessary attention to that part of your body.

Empire

The Empire is narrowest just below the bust and conceals your waist and hips. Starting the waistline beneath the bust works well for smaller busts, and the long line makes petite brides look taller. For the ultimate romantic style, this one won't let you down. The Empire line with an A-line skirt will also do a marvellous job at concealing wider hips. An Empire line with a column skirt adds height and balances a smaller bust.

Ball Gown

This style suits all brides as it disguises the body from the waist and hips down. It is flattering when worn with the right style of bodice. These skirts are worn with tulle and/or a hoop underneath. They can also be very heavily gathered or pleated at the waistline. This gives them the poof. This style of skirt can be made entirely of tulle, with no other fabric, which gives the very soft, romantic look. The bottom of each layer of tulle can also be fluted, which gives that curly effect and is really sweet when matched with the fluting on the veil. This is a somewhat younger style, but very pretty and classic nonetheless.

Sheath

This skirt is very classy and elegant; the skirt is simply fitted at the hips and falls straight down to the floor. You can have an attachment that ties around the waist like a wraparound skirt and this can be your train. This attachment can also be quite puffy so you have the effect of a princess style skirt that is straight at the front. This style will only suit the bride that has a healthy curvaceous figure. You do not necessarily need to be slim and petite, but you do need a reasonably flat stomach and backside.

Strapless A-line

The traditional version of this gown is a strapless A-line. There are now many variations whereby you can have pleats, shoulder straps, and the like. The distinct feature of the princess style gown is the fitted bodice and waist, which continue on to the A-line skirt. This style is very flattering for larger brides as it is simple and elegant, and this creates the illusion of height. However, to make it work, you need to have some bust. Likewise, going strapless is not the most appropriate option if you are big busted. And, surprisingly, if you are very petite and slim with little or no bust, it most likely will not be suitable as it simply emphasises the fact.

Why so cheap?

You get what you pay for, especially when it comes to fabric and details in bridal gowns. Usually, the more expensive the gown the better the finish and quality.

When looking at gowns with embellishments such as beading, are they **sewn or glued** on?
Is the dress **lined**?
Is the **fabric** scratchy or itchy?
Are the seams **visible**?

smart STEPS

✷ There will always be another dress. Don't be compelled to make a decision on the spot.

✷ Be like Fonzie, act cool.

✷ Make notes of style numbers and details. Research online.

✷ For many brides, a process of elimination is your best bet. Try on a range of dresses; even those you don't think will suit you.

✷ Don't be afraid of second hand gowns.

✷ Pick a dress that YOU love, that makes YOU feel fabulous. Forget trends and what looks good on waifs.

SMART WEDDING   73

SHOES

Whenever I have a conundrum my Dad says to "draw up a pros and cons list", then you have all the information "right there in front of you". Good one Dad. When it comes to wedding shoes, like most wedding related items, it's easy to spend a bomb, but hey, they're only shoes ... beautiful, leathery, sparkly, heeled, feminine ...

Look, clearly shoes are something I have a problem with. I like, no, **LOVE** shoes. They're pretty, outfit-creating things that make you tall and your calves shapely and Macpherson like ... so the big questions is, do you buy cheap shoes or spend up big on a pair of name brand designer, Carrie Bradshaw dream heels?

You might answer straight away. Nup, forget it. I'd rather have a big cake. Or perhaps you are like me, fawning over a pair of coloured Givenchy pumps that were so far out of my price range (but so deep in my heart) I bought and returned them twice. TWICE. Here's a Dad style Pros and Cons list in case you are like me.

74 SMART WEDDING

To buy or not to buy expensive shoes

PRO

They ARE gorgeous
Jessica Biel has the same pair
They are very good quality
I'll be on my feet all day
I'll definitely wear them again
My dress is long so no one will see them
It's my special day!

CON

They cost more than the cat
Jessica Biel is a millionaire
They'll probably be ruined within an hour
I'll be on my feet ALL DAY!
You probably won't wear them again
No one will see them under your dress!
You are a psycho bridezilla

I hope that clears things up for you … if not …

You can definitely purchase a 'nice' pair of shoes for under $50 (£30). But do yourself and your musculoskeletal system a favour and consider spending a couple more dollars. I hate to be Practical Patty but your wedding day is a looooong day and most of it you will be **on your feet**. You will be walking, standing, walking, jumping, walking, standing, prancing, posing, walking and then most importantly dancing!

Are the shoes a feature of the outfit? Or are they hidden between layers and layers of organza? Are the shoes a showpiece (if your dress sits above the calf then YES) or are you the only person that will ever touch/see them?

Colourful wedding shoes are quite the trend, bright gorgeous statement pieces that can change a very sedate wedding outfit into something truly sassy. Think about that. If you're safe with your dress, get some fabulous Wizard-of-Oz-style heels.

Match the shoes to your day. If you are having a casual event, like a beach ceremony on sand, then perhaps consider not wearing

SMART WEDDING   75

Step on it

www.bridalshoes.com
www.designershoes.com
www.eweddingshoes.com
www.idoshoes.com

smart STEPS

* Be comfortable. Choose shoes that won't kill you after ten minutes.
* Try on in store and then buy online.
* If you simply must wear huge heels, buy a pair of ballet flats to change into for dancing etc.

stilettos as they are both impractical and you'll probably end up crawling down the aisle. Ballet flats, fancy sandals or barefoot (yes I said it) are easier possibilities. You can wear heels later at the reception if it's on flat ground.

If you have your eye on a pair of uber **designer shoes**, Google the hell out of them. Discount shoe websites are everywhere but make sure you check the company's return policy, because shoe sizes often vary between designers and countries. Also beware of replicas and rip offs. Black Friday and post Christmas/holiday sales are a great time to score a **bargain pair** of **open toed shoes**. Payless shoes is also worth a look for simple strappy heels, and Kmart and Target both have a rather large shoe selection. If you want a specific colour, a quick and easy way is to spray-paint the shoes (silver and gold works well).

When you do buy your shoes, make sure you wear them in and around the house to avoid uncomfortable blisters and pack some Band-Aids on the day of your wedding just in case.

A bride is lucky if she wears old shoes

76   SMART WEDDING

Hair &
MAKE UP

"Kiss and make up—but too much make up has ruined many a kiss."

MAE WEST

When you stride, drift or walk down the aisle, the one person your partner is going to want to see is the *real* you, not some freaky painted over tanned doll. Sure, jazz it up a bit, but a Vegas showgirl with hair extensions, falsies (boobs and eyelashes) is probably not who your partner signed up to marry (unless you ARE a Vegas showgirl, then I apologise and please go about your business).

Professional bridal hair and make up can be pricey but getting it right, so that you feel great, is important. Good hair and make up can improve photographs and last all day but also if you are overdone it can look REALLY bad.

SMART WEDDING 77

I've worked in TV for a while and have had my hair and make up done by professional artists often. When it's done right, I think, **look and feel good** … I'm confident that I still look like me, but more even toned and with thicker lashes. Too much make up and I look like a cakey, old, bloated bag. I can say that because it's me.

You **don't** want to look like a cakey, old, bloated bag (or if you need a direct visual reference, Snookie).

That is BAD.

If you don't wear a lot of make up in your everyday life, don't wear a lot on your wedding day. You aren't playing a character, it's not Halloween or a dress up party, it's a wedding.

> *If you don't wear a lot of make up in your everyday life, don't wear a lot on your wedding day. You aren't playing a character, it's not Halloween or a dress up party, it's a wedding.*

The most obvious and **budget-friendly** option for wedding day hair and make up is DIY. If you have a regular hairdresser, you could go to them for your hair and if you are confident with your look do your own make up. Kate Middleton did her own make up for her wedding day and hey, she was marrying a prince!

Saving money on your make up for your wedding day is relatively easy. **Department store** make up artists will often work for free as long as you buy something from them. Go to counters that you would normally buy cosmetics from. If you wear Clinique, approach their counter and ask if they take make up bookings. By using a brand that your skin is familiar with, you are less likely to have any reactions to the products.

Not everyone has the skills to do their own make up so if you fear that it may be clown-like then there are a couple of options you might consider.

Most hairdressing salons have connections to make up artists. Talk to them about who they work with regularly and would recommend. Try and **negotiate** to have **hair and make up** done in the salon to cut travel time and fees. Some hairdressers are likely to charge a fee for coming to you, so if you want to save money, go to the salon. Make a morning of it. Ask if you can bring champagne and nibbles (some salons even provide this on the morning of the wedding).

smart STEPS

- If you are using a make up artist have a trial.
- Collect clippings and examples of hair and make up you wish to try.
- Always look like YOU.
- Don't go overboard.
- Steady on the spray tan.
- If you are DIY'ing hair and make up, practise, practise, practise!

Will the salon offer a **discount** if you bring the whole bridal party?

To make sure you get the look that you want on the day, most hairdressers recommend a **trial**. Some hairdressers will do it for free; others include the cost of the trial in the wedding day. Confirm this prior to the appointment.

If you are going to wear a veil, hairclip or netting, take them to your trial. On your wedding day, wear a zip up top (or something you can get over your hair and make up).

LADIES AND GENTS,
brideslaves and groomsmen

Hmmm, where to begin?

By now you've chosen whether or not you are having a bridal party and who they are. I hope you like them because they're your A team. People who you both can rely on to help you out, plan a super awesome bucks and hens party (if that's your style) and placate any pre wedding insano meltdowns that you are NOT going to have. My wish for you at this stage is a drama free build up to the big event.

Dramas usually happen when people don't get what they want. The good thing about families, in particular siblings, is they generally just tell you why they are angry and then knowing that, you can go to work fixing the problem or simply just yell back. Friends can be tricky. In a bridal party situation, you are creating a **new group dynamic**, throwing people together that perhaps haven't gelled before. There will probably be stupid power struggles (even if you aren't aware), infantile tiffs around who knows you better and who is a closer friend blah blah blah. Don't get involved with this. It's trouble. Only step in if they are going to kill each other. It's a fact that at least one bridesmaid will want the day to be about her.

Fact.

Even if they're the best chicks in the world, there will probably be some underlying issue that you must do your best to ignore.

Groomsmen also have these problems but because they are men, they tend to just hold it in for the next 28 years, when casually at their kid's graduation BBQ, one will say to the other "Gee Phil, when you picked John over me as your best man … well that was kind of harsh," and then they shake or man hug and move on.

When it comes to clothing the bridal party, well get ready, it can be a **hell of a ride**. Firstly yes, this is *your* day and what you want is important *but* you should also be aware that when dressing your nearest and dearest friends (bridesmaids, groomsmen, maid of honour etc) for your wedding that they aren't Barbie and Ken dolls. They are individual humans with their own free will. They come in all different shapes and sizes and **not everyone** is going to be **happy** with what you have envisaged for them to wear. Why must we dress everyone in the same clothes? It's tradition of course (I DARE YOU TO BREAK IT!)

Here's why …

The bridesmaid tradition originated from later Roman law, which required 10 witnesses at a wedding in order to outsmart evil spirits believed to attend marriage ceremonies (otherwise known as your future mother in-law! Boom! Sorry). The bridesmaids and ushers dressed in **identical**

> In a bridal party situation, you are creating a new group dynamic, throwing people together that perhaps haven't gelled before.

SMART WEDDING

clothing to the bride and groom, so that the evil spirits wouldn't know who was getting married.

So it has a bit of history.

Fine.

Whatevs.

I know a girl who chose her bridal party by their **body shape and size** (as in the skinny chicks) and left her best friend, who had just had a baby, off the list because she 'didn't suit the dress'. It was superficial and it sucked, denting a lifelong friendship all because she thought the photos would look better.

I wish I made that story up. **It's sad.**

Who pays for said dress or suit?

Good question. Googling this is fun and bitchy. It's a fiercely contented grey area.

Bridesmaids might say, "Hey lady, if you want me to wear that taffeta monstrosity that may or may not be a bedspread, which I will **NEVER** wear again, then you pay for it."

Brides may say, "Hey, I've held your hair while you vomited and I never acknowledge that your fake tan is too dark, give it up and buy the goddamn dress that I want ... I'd do it for you."

Having been a bridesmaid and a bride I will say both parties are right BUT it's pretty important to **discuss who's paying** for what with your bridal party before making any decisions. If the bridal party is paying for the dress/suit, then discuss a budget. Be mindful that financial situations differ and not everyone has $400+ (£255) to spend on a cocktail dress and shoes. If it's uncomfortable to talk about this with the group then discuss individually. Don't pressure or make them feel uncomfortable. Yes you want everything to look and feel right but surely your relationship is more important? If it's them paying their rent or buying your couture gown, then take that into **consideration**, for the sake of your **friendship** and them having a roof over their head (and not sleeping on your couch post wedding).

If you can afford to pay for the bridal party attire, fab, do so and then you have a little more power of persuasion. If not perhaps come to a compromise. If you

> *If the bridal party is paying for the dress/suit, then discuss a budget. Be mindful that financial situations differ and not everyone has $400+ (£255) to spend on a cocktail dress and shoes.*

are requesting that they wear the same jewellery, make up, hairstyles, cufflinks, etc, it's a nice gesture for you to pay for these additional items, or even use the jewellery, for example, as a gift for your attendants.

When looking at outfits and combinations for the bridal party, consider all of the **different body shapes** and sizes. Who will be comfortable in what and is there a possibility of the attendants being able to re-wear their dress or suit in the future? (They might be a lot more obliging on paying for the outfit if they think they will re-wear it.)

A wise choice for the ladies may be for you to select a colour/length/designer and let your bridesmaids **choose their own dresses** or if you are having the dresses made, choose the material and let the bridesmaids select their own style of dress that suits them … maybe a mini, Grecian, halter, strapless, off-the-shoulder, etc. They will be grateful to be able to select a dress cut that they are comfortable in and that flatters their bodies.

If you are going for bridesmaid dresses that are identical, head to the Internet. Websites such as **shopshop.com** and **jcrew.com** offer a wide range of simple formal gowns and dresses in lots of colours and sizes. They also offer swatches so you can purchase the same colour dresses in different sizes and cuts. If you are ordering online, allow at least 2 months for shipping, alterations and returns if necessary.

If you are ordering your wedding gown online or from a bridal boutique ask if they will discount your bridesmaids' dresses.

As with bridal attire, hit the **department stores** (and their websites), as the majority of shops have their own affordable formalwear lines and stock designer off the rack gowns for under $100 (£60).

For our wedding I wasn't interested in the identical formation, matchy matchy bridesmaids get up. I asked my bride's ladies if they would wear their favourite LBD (little black dress) and I found some gorgeous patterned pashminas that I gave them as a gift and it really tied them together without putting them under any additional financial pressure and they loved what they wore because they chose it.

This is the same for the **groomsmen's suits,** some cuts may flatter and others not. Having a key colour such as black, grey or navy may be another way to get around the bridesmaids dress saga. For more casual weddings, groomsmen can wear their own trousers and have matching shirts or ties to bring it all together. Hiring a suit is also way cheaper than buying but be mindful to book a proper fitting for the groomsmen to try on the suit. When having the suits fitted, check that they actually fit, that the collar is the correct size, the jacket can be comfortably done up and they can comfortably sit in the pants without any comical splitting or tactical separation.

Most **wedding day disasters** appear to be around men accidently wearing child sized suits or pants that are so short that they show their calves. Before picking them up double check that they are the correct suits and if time allows make sure that groomsmen try on the suits again in case they are incorrect. Finding a shop owner at 11am on a Sunday morning to exchange an ill-fitting suit is hardly an opportune problem.

Avoid hiring men's dress shoes. You probably wouldn't want to wear someone else's high heels (I know I wouldn't). Hire shoes can be **uncomfortable** and manky, so do the blokes a favour and let them wear their own dress shoes or get them to the shops to buy some new ones.

84 SMART WEDDING

Kids … never work with **children** or **animals**.

Toddlers are cute because they are mini people. It's fun to dress them up like adults because they're small and don't have the language capacity to resist. Grand wedding plans are created around children, little people who poo their pants and scream for no reason. **Think carefully** about including little ones in your ceremony because anything can and will happen; you're probably better off training a cat to be your ring bearer than your nephew. I sound like I don't love kids. I do love kids, sort of … I've just been to a few weddings where I've watched an 18-month-old stumble aimlessly down the aisle like a drunkard, dropping the ring cushion 5 metres before he reaches the groom and cries until everyone says 'ahhhhhh' and someone else takes the ring to the groom. Very rarely does this work.

Hiring a suit is also cheaper than buying but be mindful to book a proper fitting for the groomsmen.

smart STEPS

✸ For attendants, pick people you genuinely like. Forget obligation.

✸ Be honest from the get go and who is paying for what.

✸ If someone's being a troublemaker, get on top of it early. Don't let them kill the good vibes.

✸ Get the group together prior to the wedding.

When it comes to dressing tiny people, they sure do look cute in mini tuxedos and flowery dresses but realistically, the way kids grow they are never going to fit into these clothes again. Suit rental stores will often throw in the ring bearer's suit (alarm bells!) for free if you are renting the groomsmen's attire and shops like Kmart and Target have a great selection of pretty girl's dresses for under $40 (£25). The kids will love it and so will your wallet.

SMART WEDDING   85

DIY
(WITHOUT DOING IT YOURSELF)

If you want that DIY, home crafted, kitsch, vintage, Indie feel to your wedding but are completely lacking in any DIY skills, then like most wedding related things, you can buy them and take the credit. Fake DIY is easy.

Get someone else to package your almonds, or sew buntings or hand design your invitations. There is an abundance of crafty websites out there that will provide you with such worker bees and the BEST place to find over 800,000 of them is on Etsy.

Etsy.com, the global marketplace, was conceived by Rob Kalin in early 2005. A painter, carpenter and photographer, Rob found there was no viable marketplace to exhibit and sell his creations online, with other E-commerce sites having become too inundated with overstock electronics and broken appliances. Etsy is a **world of wedding suppliers,** handmade items and accessories, uniquely wonderful decorations, clothing, jewellery, photo booth supplies … you name it, Etsy's got it.

I love Etsy because you can hone in on local suppliers and find someone down the road who has a penchant for illustration and calligraphy to hand write your place cards, or locate an avid and talented knitter on the other side of the world to create specialised bespoke boleros for your bridesmaids. With over **13.5 million** listed items, you will find what you're looking for and without a shopfront many artisans have items at very reasonable prices. I can get lost on Etsy, spend hours 'favouriting' gloves and hats and stamps. It's a time sucker so make sure you do it at work.

Pinterest.com, or as I like to call it, *the place where I lost five months of my life.com* is one of my favourite wedding and design resources. With over 70 million users, there is an abundance of information, photographs

Etsy is a world of wedding suppliers, handmade items and accessories, uniquely wonderful decorations, clothing, jewellery, photo booth supplies …

My favourite DIY wedding projects are the 2 for 1s. Items that have a double purpose. Things like personalised coasters/bonbonniere/place settings.

An easy project for the DIY Bride and Groom are Washi Tape tile coasters.

What the hell is Washi Tape you ask? It's **Japanese** of course! (マスキングテープ)

Washi Tape is a craft phenomenon that started in 2006. A group of artists approached a Japanese masking tape manufacturer, Kamoi Kakoshi, asking them to manufacture colourful masking tapes. Of course they did!

In the beginning, there were 20 colours, designed to bring out the beauty of the rice paper (or washi) used to make the tape. The tapes were a smashing success with artists, crafters, scrap bookers and stationery lovers, both in Japan and internationally. With success came new colours, patterns and sizes. Now you can buy it in craft stores and even order bespoke tape online **(http://www.cutetape.com/).**

and (best of all) links back to the original source, so you don't have to spend 20 hours looking for that un-credited crystal belt you saw on an obscure design site. As a Pinterest user you can create your own online wedding pin board, borrow from others and be inspired.

If you are up for a **DIY challenge** may I suggest you do one project at a time and not over commit yourself. Pick the projects that are achievable and aren't too costly. Just because it's DIY doesn't mean it's going to be cheap. DIY can look easy, sew this, print that, papier-mâché 678 balloons. Pul-hease.

I found a website that suggested you make your own cocktail umbrellas. REALLY? How about you go to the supermarket and buy a pack of 100 for $3.99 (£2.50)? **Pick your battles.** That one my friends, well, it's not worth the time or the effort.

DIY Washi Tape coasters

These coasters are a great wedding table inclusion. They are easy and inexpensive.

You can group them together in sets to make adorable wedding favours or just use one for each guest as a coaster and place card.

What you need:
Ceramic Tiles (can be purchased in bulk at any hardware or craft store)
Washi Tape
Felt pads (stick on)
Waterproof sealer

1. Take a ceramic tile and stick your tape on in any design or pattern that you like.

2. Add a light coat of waterproof lacquer or Mod Podge (all-in-one sealer, glue and finish) over the tiles to keep the tape in place and protect it from spills or condensation.

3. Use 'em!

Pick the projects that are achievable and aren't too costly.

SMART WEDDING

Happy SNAPS

Photography can be the most costly and overpriced wedding related cost. On one hand you don't want Aunt Vera taking all of the photos and on the other you don't want to be spending $10,000 (£6,400). You have to find a balance, a happy, cash medium.

Quality photos tell the story of your day. You can have a photographer with you while you are getting ready, right until you leave the reception (but it'll cost you).

What photos are important to you?
Posed **family** shots?
The **ceremony**?
Having your **make up** done?

People boogying on the **dance** floor?

As with the celebrant or minister you need to communicate with your photographer about what shots are necessary and be perfectly clear about what **style of photography** you are after. A good wedding photographer will catch those all-important special moments and be an **unobtrusive** photo ninja while doing it.

What's your budget for wedding photography?

When selecting a professional photographer, ask to see **examples** of weddings that they have previously photographed and if you have seen photographs in magazines or on websites of the style of images that you would like at your wedding, bring them to your first meeting. If the photographer is unwilling to budge on the way they work or look at your examples, move on.

Pricing of wedding photographers, unlike other industries such as catering and cosmetics, is pretty much anyone's game. Photographers can trade the 'artistic merit' card (rightfully so) and can also quite legitimately charge you many hundreds of dollars for reprints and enlargement of your photographs.

Quality photography is a must but it isn't without negotiation.

Ask the photographer if their fee includes the **copyright** of the photos and if they are willing to provide a disc or thumb drive of the **original files.** If they won't give you the files, the photographer will own your photographs and whenever you want to send a copy to a relative or compile a photo album, you will have to go to the photographer and pay them for the shot. So on top of you already paying for their services on the day, the photographer will gain financially from your wedding until the copyright agreement ceases (can be five years or it can be forever!).

Read the contract and know your rights. Re-print fees are nasty and can be very expensive. If they won't budge on this make sure the package includes a number of reprints and be aware that they own your photos.

> *You need to communicate with your photographer about what shots are necessary and be perfectly clear about what style of photography you are after.*

SMART WEDDING   91

Professional photographers create package deals for weddings, for example a package could consist of:

+ 3 **hours** of photography, wedding service, family and group photos.
+ 50 **prints**.
+ 2 **enlargements**.
+ 1 **location shoot** with bride and groom (usually in-between the ceremony and reception).

The prices for these packages are generally between $1,500 and $3,000 (£950-1,900). Some photography packages also include an album.

If you are serious about saving money, the photographer produced wedding album should be the first to go. They cost upwards of $1,000 (£630). There are many **DIY publishing** websites that offer the same service for under $100 (£63).

Coffee table books look pretty and flashy but they will usually take a couple of months to compile and you don't always get to pick what shots are featured. You can create your own **personalised wedding album** online; adding your own captions and including ceremony notes and details.

Some sites will ask you to download the bookmaker software (for free) and others allow you to upload your images and comments directly to their site and then you can select your photographs, the layout, colour and text. You choose the style, cover and quality and within weeks you have your very own published book.

Amateur and **hobby photographers** are another option when looking for a photographer. The term amateur doesn't have to mean inexperienced, hopeless and unqualified. There are plenty of members of photography associations and adult education organisations that don't take photographs as their full time job, but are just as talented as professional photographers. Your job is to weed out the wannabes from the genuinely talented. Perhaps they are looking to quit their day job to become a full time photographer and need to up the quality of their portfolio?

Some amateur or hobby photographers are happy to shoot weddings at discounted prices and **hand over the files** at the end of the day.

You can also visit a local university or arts school's photography department and see if there are any promising future wedding photographers. Post up some notices. Look at their portfolios and ask

If you are looking for a qualified photographer look for your local Institute of Professional Photography organisation.

staff about who they might recommend. This option is a little time consuming and some would say risky but if you are unsure about their skill level, one way to test them is by asking for them to shoot some engagement photographs as a trial. If you are comfortable with the shoot and are happy with the overall product you might have scored yourself a great deal. One way to ensure everyone is happy when using a student, amateur or hobby photographer is by allowing them to use your wedding photographs in **their portfolio**. A small but helpful gesture from you to help them get more work in the future.

Another bargaining tool for photography and many other aspects of the day is the time of year that you choose to hold your wedding. In summer business may be booming for wedding vendors, but if your wedding is held at a quieter time of year you may have more **bargaining power** due to lack of business on their part. If they need your business, they will budge and pander to your needs and special requests.

Another bargaining tool for photography is the time of year that you choose to hold your wedding.

VIDEOGRAPHY

Have you been forced to watch a friend's or relative's wedding video under duress? Boring hey? Yep.

You wouldn't tell them that but no matter how high the production values are it's never quite as good as being there.

Videography is a tricky decision for many couples.

The first question when thinking about whether it is worth the **cost** is, realistically how many times would you anticipate watching your **wedding video** (or making friends and relatives sit through it?).

There are pros to having a wedding video made; maybe you want to watch it for things you missed, relive your vows, or to try and remember the name of your cousin's ex-girlfriend. But is it worth **$3,000 (£1,900)**? That is the average price of a professional videographer. As well as the cost, it can take months and months to get the finished product back to you after editing.

Enquire at your local University; many have a media department full of students who are experts on shooting and editing video or better yet, see if there's a specialised film school in your area.

If you do hire a professional, choose a **simple package** that doesn't include a lot of special effects or editing. Hire them for the ceremony, and maybe for a part of the reception. The majority of a videographer's fee comes from editing, so another way to save money is to just get the raw footage from them. You can always have it edited further down the track. A more cost effective option is to have a friend or family member with some experience using a video camera film the wedding. You can **rent or borrow** a video camera if you don't already have one or even, dare I say, use an iPhone.

smart STEPS

✱ Always insist on owning complete copyright of images.

✱ Decide on the style of photographs and how you want the photography to work PRIOR to the wedding day.

✱ Create a list of 'must have shots'.

✱ Show the photographer examples of the style of poses etc you wish to have covered.

✱ Don't scrimp on photography but DO shop around and get value for money.

✱ Don't pay for photographer's albums. Make your own. They are a RIP OFF.

$3000 (£1,900) is the average price of a professional videographer.

SMART WEDDING

The business end:
INVITATIONS

So, you've organised this shindig, probably come to blows over who is attending and now you've got to tell people about it … it's invitation time.

> SAVE THE DATE!
> We're tying The Knot!
> Joseph popped the question and Belinda said yes.
> Please join us on June 17, 2014
> Bondi Beach, New South Wales. Invitation to follow.

When you send the invitations is much disputed … Google it!

Etiquette crazies love this topic. Personally, I think when you send out the invitations has a lot to do with where and when the wedding is to take place. The more you are asking of your guests, the more heads up you need to give them.

If you are expecting guests to **travel** to your wedding, whether it's interstate or overseas, you'll need to give them **a bit of notice** (and detailed information) so that they can take time off work and plan travel and accommodation. Give them six to eight months notice before the wedding (especially if you are asking them to take a pricey trip).

Save the date cards are a cool idea but the pessimist in me says "hey, this is another expense that has crept into wedding planning must dos".

Save the Date cards, magnets, balloons (not kidding) are pretty common. They serve a purpose, especially if you have guests that live interstate or overseas or if you are planning to ask your guests to travel vast distances (and therefore spend a lot of money!). It's a heads up. Save the date cards are usually sent out **six to 12 months** in advance of invitations and allow your guests to know the time and date of your upcoming wedding so they can book travel and accommodation and make sure they don't plan something un-cancellable on your wedding day.

There's no need to spend a lot of money on preparing Save the Dates, especially if you are yet to decide on a theme or colour scheme, just keep them **simple**. One way to send out Save the Date cards, which is free, is to **email** (contentious I know). There are lots of easy to use template based html cards that look professional and stylish and are minimal cost, if not free.

Sending an **e-card** is a quick way to get the message across. If however, you have lots of technophobes in your family or friendship group, you might want to print cards and send them out. One of the fashionable Save the Date cards is a **fridge magnet**. You can order them online or if you are feeling crafty, print the cards at home, purchase a magnetic sticky strip from a local craft store and stick a 2 cm strip on the back of your card and hey presto an easy (and cheap) fridge Save the Date card.

> **NOTE:** You can't un-send a Save the Date. Finalise the guest list prior to sending because once they're out there, you're then obliged to send them an invitation.

'Standard' wedding invitations are sent out six to eight weeks before the wedding, with an **RSVP** date around 2 weeks before the day itself. If you have a sneaky reserve guest list, people on the B list that you want to try to invite if some guests can't make it, factor that timing in too. If you have a **reserve list**, it might be a good idea to send your invitations out around 3 months before the wedding. This will give any guests that can't come time to reply, and for you to issue a new wedding invite to your reserve list without them feeling like they were a last minute choice.

While you like to imagine that your wedding invitation will be **received with joy**, your guests fawning over every detail and word, think back to the last time you received a wedding invitation … how long do you spend actually looking at it? Was it immediately stuck to a pin board or refrigerator? How long do you hold it, admiring and appreciating the work and effort that has gone into to sticking the 84 individual diamantes around the outer edge of the border?

About **35 seconds** yeah?

Enough to say, "These are gaudy, I bet they were expensive" or "WHY ARE THEY GETTING MARRIED ON A FRIDAY?" or "Isn't her fiancé called Peter?"

I jest.

My point is, as much effort as you put into the invitations, it's unlikely that all of your guests will appreciate it. The main goal of the invitation is to convey information. **Who, where, when?** You don't need 18 separate cards and sections. The wedding invitation is the first opportunity (unless you've sent a Save the Date) that you have to convey to your guests the **tone** and **style** of your upcoming event. If you are having a classic formal wedding, express that to your guests with an appropriately coloured and worded invitation. If it's a rockabilly wedding, get that theme going early, have fun with it, use colour etc.

Tradition dictates embossed cards, folded or otherwise often in shades of white and ivory with fancy cursive writing in black or metallic print. These are great if your wedding is a formal affair, but too often couples choose 'swirly invitations' for informal weddings. If your wedding is in a surf club, perhaps lose the stuffy invitations and instead opt for a contemporary and unique design and wording that conveys the tone as being more relaxed.

> *Think back to the last time you received a wedding invitation … how long do you spend actually looking at it? Was it immediately stuck to a pin board or refrigerator?*

98   SMART WEDDING

Wedding invitations: What's What?

Engraved
Engraving is the most traditional form of wedding invitation printing, and one of the most expensive. Text is etched onto a copper plate, which is then coated with ink and wiped clean, leaving the ink only in the indentations. Soft, high-quality paper is pressed hard against the plate, causing it to deform into the etchings. You can tell true engraving by the "bruise" or dent on the back of the paper.

Thermography
Thermography was developed as a less expensive alternative to engraving. The printer uses ink and a powder resin combined with heat to reproduce the raised lettering effect of engraving. The text has a shiny finish and is often said to not be as sharp as engraving.

Letterpress
This old-fashioned technique has had a massive revival! A letterpress printer presses inked letters (or patterns) into a piece of paper, forming an indented surface. By repeating the process, you can create images with more than one colour.

Embossing or Blind Embossing
Most often used for small insignias and monograms, this process creates a raised impression on paper by running the paper through two metal sheets. When no ink is used, it is called "blind" embossing.

Offset Printing
Most modern printing is offset printing, also known as lithography. From magazines to postcards, this flat style of printing is a familiar one, and appropriate for an informal wedding invitation. Traditionally, an inked image is transferred from an inked plate to a rubber "blanket", which is then passed over the paper.

Invitation designing is fun and if you are up to a bit of gluing, designing and cutting, you could save yourself some big bucks and bring a **personal touch** to your invitations. Saying that, you can of course purchase pre made DIY style invitations and save yourself some long nights with the guillotine and paper cuts by buying from a local designer or an Etsy seller.

DIY invitation making doesn't necessarily mean taking a calligraphy course and handwriting 148 invitations. You can purchase basic blank invitation for your home printer from stationery supply shops, Esty and eBay. An embosser, Washi Tape or vellum paper can dress up invitations and you can even purchase a small letterpress kit with pre-designed and printed patterns, borders and logos.

Font websites like dafont.com and abstractfonts.com are a great place to source free fonts that can help you create a customised look with all of your wedding stationery from place cards to coasters, menus, or thank-you notes. Use simple fonts like Kontor serif or Lane sans serif for the elegant and modern look or Frenchy or Fragment core for something more casual and fun.

Before committing to a DIY project to save money, think about the **time and effort** that is going to go into this project and the cost of all of the tools to make it happen. I am the first to admit that I get quickly carried away with crafty missions

The fancier and more detailed heavy invitations are, with jackets, bows, buttons and embellishments, the more expensive they get. Sure, they can look nice (some ridiculously overdone), but those little extra details **can really add up**. Not only will you pay for printing, there are usually additional assembly fees (or extra work for you). Instead go for the **classic** look of a simple invitation printed on a **high-quality paper**. Cut the bells and whistles because it's highly likely that they just end up in the recycling pile or lost in a sea of 'when is it acceptable to throw this out?' documents.

that are going to save me both time and money. I'm pretty handy but even still, 95% of my projects come in over budget and I am left with tools and implements that I will never use again ... scrapbooking scissors with decorative edges anyone?

Pick your projects ... ask yourself, is it worth spending every night for three weeks cutting and gluing and getting angry at staplers to save $50 (£31)? Your **time is valuable**, particularly in the months leading up to your wedding, and ultimately, wouldn't you rather be relaxed and having a wine rather than having a breakdown over folding paper. I'm all up for DIY, just know what you are in for before buying all of the gear.

Including a prompt for **RSVP** with your invitation is important, whether you ask your guests to email or call you or include a lightweight return card (such as a postcard). You can choose to pre stamp the RSVP then all guests have to do is pop it in the post box (the easier you make it the more likely that they will return it and thus saving you time having to contact people). Make the invitations as **small and light** as possible, with minimal inserts, to save on postage.

For a postage estimate, take a complete wedding invitation to the post office for a weigh in. Include response cards, registry cards, maps and any other inserts you plan to send to your guests. Local and overseas postage costs vary depending on the thickness of the wedding invitation as well as its weight and size. Square envelopes will cost more to post than regular rectangle-shaped envelopes. Again you don't want to spend $5.00 (£3) posting the invites; because if you have 120 guests that's an extra $600 (£380). (You may think I'm being dramatic here but postage price jumps are steep.)

Remember to order **thank you notes**. This can be the most overlooked task in the wedding but it's really important. It lets your guests know how appreciative you are that they shared in your wonderful event.

We went online post wedding and created a postcard style thank you card, with a wedding photo on one side and a blank over side to write a **personalised** thank you message. As you receive gifts or contributions to your wedding registry, keep a check list of who gave what (trust me on this).

When writing a thank you card, the basic formula is to express gratitude, be specific about the gift, and thank them for

> Make the invitations as small and light as possible, with minimal inserts, to save on postage.

SMART WEDDING

attending (or for thinking of you if they could not attend).

Perhaps tell the giver how you will use the gift. For example, "We used the blender for post wedding margaritas. It's awesome."

If the gift is cash or a registry contribution, thank them for their generosity without mentioning a specific amount.

WEDDING INVITATION WORDING

I have received many a formal wedding invitation with how do you say … wanky wording. **Wording** that often doesn't **match the occasion**. Using "The honour of your presence" or anything with the word "cordially" in it can sometimes come across as stuffy and a bit unnecessarily posho. I mean, if you speak like that in real life, then go for it. If you are royalty, right on, but if you are a regular gorgeous couple, you don't have to be swept up in literary pompousness, say what you want to say, how you want to say it. Announce your plans for the future with a wedding invitation that captures the joy you feel.

Wording wedding invitations doesn't have to be tricky. Select words that reflect your **love and happiness**. Make it playful.

There are some schools of thought (that are pretty traditional) that like to include both parents' names at the beginning of the invitation, especially if the parents are paying for and/or (formally hosting) the event, although in the end, this decision is up totally up to you.

Typically, the wedding invitation will include the following details:

✦ **Who** is hosting the wedding (e.g. the parents of bride, groom, both, or the bride and groom themselves)
✦ Name/s of the **guest/s**
✦ **Location**, full date and year
✦ **Time** of the ceremony
✦ **Reception** information
✦ **Dress** code
✦ **RSVP** information
✦ **Contact** details

Keeping your message short will also make it more powerful and will likely have the best effect on its intended recipients.

Betty Bride
&
Gene Groom
are getting married

Please join us for the celebration on November 5th, 2014 at 3:00pm the Colgate Divinity School 640 Bay Drive, Kingston.

He asked…
And she said Yes!

Betty Bride
&
Gene Groom
are getting married.

Please join us for the celebration on
November 5th, 2014
at 3:00pm
the Colgate Divinity School
640 Bay Drive,
Kingston.

smart STEPS

✴ The less complicated and classic the invitation, the more value for money they will be.

✴ Most guests will read and bin. Remember that when you are designing and paying for them.

✴ Save money by creating a wedding webpage which includes details, instructions and maps.

✴ Think about the formality of the invitation and what message you want them to convey.

Mr & Mrs Michael Smith together request the pleasure of the company of guest's name at the marriage of their daughter
Betty Bride
to
Gene Groom
at Colgate Divinity School
640 Bay Drive,
Kingston
on Saturday, November 5th, 2014
at 3:00pm and afterwards at
Fancy Manor, Fitzroy.

Personalised WEB PAGES

A very modern wedding addition is creating your own wedding website. You don't have to be a coding genius or know anything about html to create your own site. Just Googling 'wedding website' brings up hundreds if not thousands of companies that offer free templates and limited hosting for your personalised site.

Without being too vacuous, having a page 'all about you', wedding websites can be **very useful**, particularly if you are having out of town guests attend or if your wedding is a destination event. By preparing a suggested **accommodations** and attractions page, you can help your guests plan ahead of time and make their trip as worry-free and as enjoyable as possible. If you are holding pre-wedding and post wedding events, if you need to add maps and **directions**, a wedding events and info page can be a much cheaper option than adding multiple inserts into the printed invitation.

By adding the website address to the invitation you can also manage **RSVP** lists via the site, meal preferences and any special requests for the event and then export the information straight to a spreadsheet.

DIY NAME CARDS

Our wonderful stationery designer Samone from Cake Ink came up with some great little name cards that also conveyed a little of our sense of humour.

Using a simple pegboard, she attached gorgeous printed tags, which featured the guest's name and table number and on the opposite side a little love quote.

Here are 10 of my favourites.

"I don't think I'll get married again. I'll just find a woman I don't like and give her a house."
LEWIS GRIZZARD

"Whatever you may look like, marry a man your own age — as your beauty fades, so will his eyesight."
PHYLLIS DILLER

"I spent a lot of money on booze, birds and fast cars. The rest I just squandered."
GEORGE BEST

"I think men who have a pierced ear are better prepared for marriage. They've experienced pain and bought jewellery."
RITA RUDNER

"It's not the men in my life that count, it's the life in my men."
MAE WEST

"Women will never be as successful as men because they have no wives to advise them."
DICK VAN DYKE

"A man in love is incomplete until he has married. Then he's finished."
ZSA ZSA GABOR

"A good wife always forgives her husband when she's wrong."
MILTON BERLE

"I never mind my wife having the last word. In fact, I'm delighted when she gets to it."
WALTER MATTHAU

"Never go to bed mad. Stay up and fight."
PHYLLIS DILLER

SMART WEDDING

HENS & Bucks NIGHTS

OK, chances are if you are reading this, you are probably a bride (no judgment grooms) and traditionally organising the hens night and bridal shower is done by bridesmaids or the maid of honour; saying that, there is nothing wrong with organising your own or doing it as a group.

If you are leaving the organising of the day/evening/weekend to a bridesmaid, groomsman or friend let them know what you want. **Be clear** on exactly the type of party or event you would like and who you would like to attend. Give the organiser a list of friends with their contact details and then leave it in their capable hands.

Why do we go on these nights?

To **bond**?
To get **smashed**?
To walk around in **god-awful veils** and phallic necklaces?
To have a last crazy, **sexual hurrah**?*

*If you answered last hurrah, then please rethink the wedding.

Hens and bucks nights can be anything from a dinner and drinks with friends to a completely mental *Hangover* style adventure, with tigers and shaved heads. It's whatever you want it to be and can be a great way for all of your friends from different worlds (work, family, uni) to get together and connect before the big day. All eyes will be **on you** for the evening, **so indulge**! Revel in the party spirit and remember everyone is there to celebrate with you. If your friend's plans involve dressing you in a silly outfit then go with it, as long as it has a crotch; they just want it to be unforgettable (also remember you are an autonomous being so if you don't feel comfortable doing something speak up).

Coupon websites are a great place to find discount dining, accommodation and activity deals for Hens and Bucks nights.

Enjoy the surprises and don't give in to temptation and probe your friends for details on the event, it will only spoil the plans and the overall effect of what your girlies and blokes have in store for you.

Don't opt to hold the hens and bucks celebrations **the night before** the wedding, I would strongly advise against this. This is asking for trouble. Try to plan for the hens and bucks nights to occur **at least a week out** from your wedding day to have some recovery time and so you aren't stressed by last minute organisational tasks that may be on your mind. Some couples like to combine the hens night and bridal shower into one day, if you are restricted by time, having the bridal shower in the afternoon at home and then heading out for dinner and dancing afterwards can keep all of your female guests, no matter what age, happy.

There are plenty of activities that are fun, inexpensive and a little on the alternative side.

- Organise a bridal themed scavenger hunt.
- Visit an **art gallery** followed by a posh boozy lunch.
- Create a delicious bridal **brunch**.
- Host a **dinner party** and ask all guests to bring a dish, pick a theme to make it easier.
- Jump aboard a **winery** tour.
- Create a **theme** for the day such as chocolate, tour a chocolate factory and then go to an ice cream parlour and eat chocolate sundaes followed by chocolate cocktails at a bar! Then vom.
- Partake in a **high tea**.
- If it is **racing** season, get dressed up and head out for a flutter!
- Host a **'who done it?'** murder weekend.

If you can't afford a day at a spa, have your own beauty at home day. Make face masks, use foot spas, paint your nails (good wedding day preparation) and make cocktails.

BRIDAL SHOWERS
& Cellar Parties (AKA FREE STUFF)

Nannas love bridal showers. They usually don't contain too many penis references and it gives them an opportunity to make cakes and for us to eat them. Don't deny anyone that. Although they might go against the foundations of feminism and can be naff, bridal showers are fab for getting free stuff for the kitchen that you have been avoiding or couldn't warrant spending the money on for years.

Unlike hens nights, where you invite your nearest and dearest friends, bridal showers are a good opportunity to invite the 'outer circle' including annoying relatives, second cousins and mothers-in-laws.

An etiquette guide from the 1920s suggested showers should be "purely spontaneous and informal," with guests arriving unannounced at the bride-to-be's home.

This is my worst nightmare. I hate the pop in. They should be banned.

Nowadays bridal showers are hosted at home at a specific invited time and a **meal or afternoon tea** is served. Adding a bit of booze to the afternoon can also make things fun … half a glass of champagne and Aunty Mary will reveal all.

I never thought I would say this but a professionally hosted bridal shower is also

> *Bridal showers were meant to strengthen the ties between the bride and her friends, provide her moral support, and help her prepare for her marriage. Gift giving at showers dates from the 1890s.*

an option. This is not as bad as it sounds and it isn't a scam. Organisations like Tupperware will arrange for a representative to come to your home and throw a party. Basically it is just like a normal Tupperware party but for hosting the party the bride gets all of the commission gift vouchers and guests can buy her items out of the catalogue. They also arrange for party games to be played. If you need re-sealable items and like leftovers, then this may be an option for you.

A gourmet-themed **tasting shower**, wine, chocolate or cheese is also a great option. Get the professionals in or do it yourself.

For gifts, pick a theme like glassware or bake-ware. If you've always wanted a Kitchen Aid mixer or blender this would be the perfect opportunity to suggest it as a gift for your shower.

> *The wedding shower originated with a Dutch maiden who fell in love with an impoverished miller. Her friends "showered" her and her groom with many gifts so the couple could do without her dowry.*

110 SMART WEDDING

CELLAR PARTIES

If you like wine, then you're about to hit the jackpot.

Cellar parties are becoming popular as an alternative to bucks and hens nights or as an addition to the pre-wedding celebrations. At the end of the party, your wine cellar will be FULL. Full I tell you. It's pretty simple. You invite guests, both male and female, to a party at to your house and ask them to **bring a bottle** of wine. Serve some cheese and snacks, open a couple of bottles and at the end of the party, you have enough wine to last you a year. Another nice idea is to keep the bottle for when the guest comes over to your house in the future to share with them! It's a nice idea but let's face it, if you're like me, that wine will be gone pronto.

smart STEPS

* If you don't want strippers and party busses then speak up.

* If the night is going to get messy, then perhaps don't invite Grandma.

* Hens and Bucks don't have to cost a mint, don't forget the budget when planning these events.

* If you don't want or need Tupperware or home accessories, pick a different theme for showers etc.

Wedding day
TRANSPORT

If your ceremony and reception are at the same venue; firstly, well done you and secondly, if you genuinely want to save money, do yourself a favour and skip right past any specialised wedding car services.

Arriving at your wedding in a flashy old vintage car that you paid $900 (£574) to hire (for probably an hour) and no one will see you in is one of the biggest wedding day **rip offs**. Cars are an expensive and often unnecessary addition to the wedding day bill. If you're having a church wedding, all of your guests will be inside the church, **who is going to witness** your grand arrival? The driver? Sure, you don't want to turn up to the wedding in an old clapper but looking at alternative options will be a guaranteed money saver.

When it comes to limos, well, Jerry Seinfeld pretty much sums up my feelings:

"You know what I never get with the limo? The tinted windows. Is that so people don't see you? Yeah, what a better way not to have people notice you than taking a thirty foot Cadillac with a TV antenna and a uniformed driver. How discreet. Nobody cares who's in the limo. You see a limo go by, you know it's either some rich jerk or fifty prom kids with $1.75 each."

Sorry limo lovers but limos are tacky … and so are Hummers. Unless you're going for Jersey Shore themed nuptials then I say avoid. They're gaudy and bit vomitus. They have a **high price tag** due to all the unnecessary extras that come with them. Do you really need an eight-passenger limo with a television, flashing lights, full sound systems with subwoofers for just yourself and your bridal party?

Chauffers, private car services and sleek black sedans are far **more affordable** and are unassuming and classic.

You could also consider a regular hire car. Ask a friend or relative to be the driver. Shopping around, there are always good deals for daily rates and a lot of rental companies have snazzier cars such as convertibles and high-end vehicles for the same hire rate as a Toyota Camry. As a bonus, you can also attain frequent flyer points with car hire rentals and remember to check if they have any deals going for members.

Guest transportation is not a necessity. Most guests wouldn't expect transport to be included. But if you are having your reception and ceremony in an out of the way location and you are conscious about your guests drink driving, there are inexpensive and fun ways of getting your guests from one place to another. You could rent a party bus or double-decker bus.

If you are renting vehicles with drivers, only have them drop you off and pick you up at the location. Why should you pay for the driver to **sit around** in the car park for six hours while you're at the reception?

Some car rental companies may say that you need to book for a minimum of three hours for a wedding. **Don't tell them** that it is for a **wedding**. Just say you need a car to pick up "X" number of people at a certain time, and then come back to pick you up later on. If they aren't buying it, book with separate companies if necessary.

You can also look into a classic car club in your area and see if you can hire one of their members to drive you and your bridal party. You can also rent an older car, like a Mustang or a convertible and drive yourselves, or simply use your own car. No one is going to remember the car; it's the person in it that counts!

smart STEPS

✹ If no one is going to see you in a fancy car, ditch it.

✹ Check overtime costs with the chauffeur company in case there are unplanned delays.

✹ If you have a non drinking generous friend, ask them to be your wedding day driver.

✹ If you must have a 'fancy car' use it for the arrival or departure only.

> If you are renting vehicles with drivers, only have them drop you off and pick you up at the location.

Let me ENTERTAIN YOU

My favourite wedding moment was dancing hard ... kicking off my heels, going barefoot and trotting gleefully around dance floor with our family and friends, who were all grooving and swaying to the music in their own individual, funky ways.

We had an amazing DJ, Andy McClelland, who just got us. I danced until he pulled the power plug and it was unadulterated joy. We'd pulled it off, the wedding was in full swing, our guests appeared to be having **a cracking time** and I wasn't going to miss out on a moment of it. Sure I probably should have talked to people more, worked the room, but how often do you get to look and feel that good and totally own the dance floor? I'd love to say every weekend but …

SMART WEDDING 115

That elusive "fun factor" inevitably rides with the vibe of your **wedding entertainment**. Of course, like everything having to do with weddings, the high price tag of wedding entertainment can intimidate the budget conscious couple. You don't need to fly in Elton John or Gaga to make it awesome, you just need to know your market … what floats your boat? What do you call a good time?

Think about your guests. Are they old? Young? Will they dance? **What mood do you want to create?** If you have decided on a renaissance recreation wedding, a local punk band might not be that appropriate. Do you want live music, or would an iPod suffice?

If you are programming your own playlist, think about what sort of music the **majority of your guests** want to hear. Of course it is your day but if you want the audience to get up and dance, playing a Radiohead album (no matter how brilliant it may be) is probably not going to be a dance floor winner. If choosing your own music sounds too stressful, perhaps a DJ would be fitting.

The DJ business is pretty competitive and portable sound systems have made it a compact affair. The benefits of a **professional DJ** are that it takes the pressure off you. They should have a good idea about what sort of music to play to get people up and dancing and what's the right background music for meal service.

Like all wedding vendors and service providers, it pays to shop around and ask friends and family if they have suggestions.

Negotiate a start time with the DJ that gives you maximum **dancing and entertainment** opportunities. Maybe you could pre program some background music and have the DJ start later, closer to dancing time? Let them set their gear up prior to the reception and arrange a time for them to return and get the party started!

Live bands and orchestras can be expensive. A smaller band equals a smaller cost for you. If you know you want a jazz band, instead of a small orchestra, go for

Think about your guests. Are they old? Young? Will they dance? What mood do you want to create? Do you want live music, or would an iPod suffice?

116   SMART WEDDING

book ahead, especially if your wedding is in peak wedding season (spring/summer).

Some popular bands, like reception venues, can be booked out **well in advance**, so make sure when you find entertainment you like, pay a securing deposit as soon as possible. If you are lost when looking for a band, check out your local entrainment guide in the newspaper. Go along and see some of their gigs and approach the band on the night for prices and availability. Don't book a band purely by reputation. They might totally suck and mess with your wedding day vibe.

Ceremony musicians such as string quartets and soloists can be pretty pricey, sometimes charging $500-$1,000 (£320-660). If your music budget is tight then I would suggest ditching the ceremony music or thinking of an alternative. The ceremony is about you and your partner and the ceremony musicians will only really play a couple of pieces, as you arrive and leave.

a trio or quintet! Or using the same idea as the DJ, hire the band for cocktail hour and the first dances, then switch to an iPod or a DJ for the rest of the reception. Make sure when you are booking the band or DJ that you prearrange the times that you wish the band to set up their gear and how long each set will go for. Also make sure you are paying them a **set rate** and ascertain if there are any hidden fees such as overtime that they may try and pull on you on the night. If your wedding is on a Friday or Saturday night,

The most money ever spent on a wedding singer was £2 million to secure Elton John's services.

SMART WEDDING

If your ceremony site has a quality sound system, why not buy or borrow some classical CDs and get someone reliable to **cue the music**. Or if you have musical friends, why not ask them to perform during the ceremony? It's a win win, you get a couple of free songs and they feel included and special.

Does your local university have a conservatorium of music? This is a great place to find talented, qualified and inexpensive musicians. Music teachers and department heads can recommend the best students in the course and any emerging ensembles that may be worth taking a look at.

Of course, when weighing up all the costs of a wedding, you may decide that you want to spend your budget elsewhere entirely.

However, it's worth bearing in mind that one of the things **guests remember** most about a wedding is the entertainment. Fantastic live music during a reception, or a skilled DJ will delight your guests and keep them talking about your wedding and your dance floor moves for months (well that's what I tell myself anyway).

smart STEPS

✷ Decide if you want a live band or DJ and shop around. Go to gigs and ask for references.

✷ Confirm any additional costs for hire of gear, transport and overtime.

✷ If the party is really going off, will they stay longer?

✷ Use contacts and recommendations.

> If your ceremony site has a quality sound system, borrow some classical CDs and get someone reliable to cue the music.

Bonbonniere

Stop.

Let's be sensible.

I've been to a lot of weddings and there's no nice way to say this ... but I've received a lot ... a LOT of crappy, forgettable bonbonniere and gifts that I know probably cost the couple a packet and that I promptly threw away or left in a hotel room.

This is where things can get really out of hand when it comes to money. Some couples go nuts when it comes to this part of the reception. Here's an idea. Instead of giving guests almonds or personalised, handmade iced cookies, just put all of the money you were going to spend in a big bucket and burn it.

Too much?

Probably.

SMART WEDDING

Bonbonniere or **wedding favours** are small gifts given as a gesture of appreciation or gratitude to guests from the bride and groom, usually given during the wedding reception.

They are often tacky or overly smooshy … can coolers and personalised mixed CDs anyone?

If you're on a tight budget, this is the easiest thing to get rid of. Many guests leave the reception without even taking their gifts home with them.

Who **really needs** a scented monogrammed candle or a key ring? If you are looking for a personalised touch, bake some biscuits or sweets and repackage them with a copy of the recipe. Rather than spending up big on floral centrepieces, display your bonbonniere in the centre of the table and allow your guests to take them home at the end of the night. A collection of small vases with individual flowers, vibrant lollipops, or jars filled with colourful chocolates will add zest to the table and serve two purposes.

Traditionally, five **JORDAN ALMONDS** (sugar coated almonds) were presented in a confection box or wrapped in elegant fabric to represent fertility, longevity, wealth, health and happiness. The bitterness of the almond and the sweetness of the coated candy exemplify the bitter sweetness of a marriage.

FORTUNE COOKIES are another inexpensive gift. You can buy them at the supermarket or in bulk at Chinese specialties stores and on eBay. You can even order custom fortunes from a website such as customfortunecookies.com.

A 'living thing' bonbonniere such as a seedling in a jar or a packet of seeds to take home and plant can be nice. Again these **plants** can also act as part of your wedding table decorations, adding variety, colour and life to each table and eliminating the need for centrepieces. Choose from a variety of plants such as lucky bamboo, succulents, cacti, yuccas, pot belly figs and ponytails. All are hearty and hard to kill. Head to your local nursery or hardware shop and try and negotiate a deal on some bulk seedlings. That way people can go home and plant a little piece of you! (Just check that your guests won't be travelling interstate because some states will not allow plant or animal matter across their borders.)

Another unique and meaningful gift for your wedding guests could be for you to **donate** the money you would have spent on bonbonniere to an organisation that needs it. You can even create a little card telling your guests about the donation. Not to guilt trip or anything but it's better than burning your money in a bucket!

If you're on a tight budget, wedding favours are the easiest thing to get rid of. Many guests leave the reception without even taking their gifts home with them.

GIMME GIMME GIMME ...

Gifts & Honeymoon

If you want a way to avoid the inevitable selections of George Foreman Grills, Foot Spas and all of the other useless junky items that friends and family kindly unload on you as wedding gift then perhaps telling them what you would like will help guide them to making the right purchase that you will love, not loath.

The easiest way to avoid bad gifts is by creating a **gift registry** or wedding list. Traditionally couples chose a retailer, usually a department or home wares store, and then created a list of desired items that was then shared with guests so as not to double up. There has been a recent trend towards gift list services that allow the couple to add almost anything to their gift list (usually called a universal registry), such as contributions to their honeymoon, flights or experience days, as well as traditional gifts from any store. Websites such as **notanothertoaster.com** specialises in providing couples with a template for their very own wedding, honeymoon or gift registry online. Guests can then collectively contribute towards larger non-conventional gifts, luxury items, honeymoon experiences, home renovations, charity groups or a combination of all of these and more. The company supplies couples with registry cards for their guests and they also have other distribution methods for guests who are not good with computers.

Although **wishing wells** (where people post envelopes of money as gifts into the well) are still popular, some couples feel uncomfortable asking directly for money as a gift. With registries you can choose for contributions to go towards something you really need. I have friends who **purchased their first home** together before the wedding and instead of gifts asked guests to contribute to their kitchen renovation. After completion they had a big 'Thank you for building our kitchen party'. It was fabulous and knowing that we helped them create something that they really loved was thanks enough.

The **average contribution** to gift registries is between $85 and $150 (£55-95) per person. If you have 100 people attending your wedding and 75 people contribute $70 (£45) you will have $5,250 (£3,350) in your registry account. That would pay for an amazing getaway or a new couch.

Now onto the **honeymoon**. The thrifty wench in me says skip the honeymoon, save the coin. But then the REAL me says take off, live in luxury, enjoy it because after all that organising and money saving, you'll need it, trust me.

The average contribution to gift registries is between $85 and $150 (£55-95) per person. If you have 100 people attending your wedding and 75 people contribute $70 (£45) you will have $5,250 (£3,350) in your registry account.

On a budget you've got a couple of options, you can:

- Work the **cost** of the honeymoon into your original budget.
- Honeymoon **at home** … spend some time on the couch and visit restaurants and local attractions that you've never gotten around to seeing.
- Use **frequent flyer** points to plan your great escape. Collect away and book ahead of time as airlines offer limited seats and they are often red-eye and early morning flights, but you can score amazing deals.
- Ask friends and family if they have a **holiday cottage**, house or shack available to rent or borrow.
- Join a holiday **home swap** community online and arrange a house swap at home or overseas (plan ahead with this one). Homelink.org has been running since 1953 and represents home swappers in 27 countries and with over 13,000 homes on the list you are sure to find somewhere fabulous. It's safe and you could stay somewhere exotic and out of your price range if you had to pay for it.

Discount voucher sites such as Groupon.com offer excellent deals on hotels, restaurants and accommodation. Again forethought and planning are needed but there are **deals to be had**. Always read the terms and conditions before buying the deal and check airfares and contact the hotels or resort to check availability. One trap of these vouchers is that they are often peak season deals so airfares can be very expensive. Check Tripadvisor.com for reviews and photographs of the accommodation facilities.

Subscribe to **travel deal websites** and keep an eye out for partnership deals with airlines and accommodation companies with packages and special discounts. Travel sites like Kayak.com allow you to search for flights based on factors that can significantly alter prices, such as the number of stops or time of day. By purchasing tickets for a red-eye or multi-stop flight, you can save hundreds on airfares. Beware of 'all inclusive deals'.

When dealing with travel agents, airlines and hotels tell **EVERYONE** that you are a newlywed. It makes you an instant **VIP**. Often hotels will gift you a bottle of champagne or a gift basket and complimentary upgrades are also a possibility.

smart STEPS

✱ If you plan to pay for the honeymoon, add it to your original budget.

✱ If you can't afford a honeymoon, plan for a big first anniversary trip.

✱ Utilise online deals and airline sales.

✱ Collect and use frequent flyer/shopper deals. Book ahead as these seats and rooms often book out, months in advance.

✱ Use a honeymoon gift registry to avoid receiving gifts that you don't want or already have.

Work the cost of the honeymoon into your original budget.

Go forth and CONQUER

Well my wedding planning Jedis that is all the knowledge I can bestow on you. Look, I'm sure there's more but the biggest piece of advice I can give you is have a bloody cracking, bonza of a day.

Don't let the little mistakes or issues (that are bound to happen) get you down, don't be an A-hole and make sure to **take it all in**.

Whether this is your first wedding, or your third, whether you're marrying a boy or a girl, whether it's a big event or small, your wedding will be the most fantastic event because **YOU** planned it and you're marrying your special person.

Make use of the generosity and love of family and friends, they want to help you wherever they can.

Don't panic, breathe and **be proud** of yourselves for pulling this whole day together!

THINGS TO REMEMBER!

✦ *Go into every meeting like it's an international negotiation.*
✦ *You're smart and you won't be beaten.*
✦ *Be prepared to walk away (if it's just a bluff).*
✦ *Repeat after me, "It's just a party. We won't come out the other end in debt."*
✦ *Remember when it's all done and dusted to write thank you notes to your guests!*

Count it down: Wedding timeline

6 months before wedding
Set budget
Compile guest list and organise addresses
Choose wedding date
Book ceremony and reception sites
Choose bridesmaids and groomsmen
Order dress and accessories, including veil and shoes
Book celebrant
Book caterer
Order wedding cake
Book florist or contact wholesale florist
Book music for ceremony and reception
Book photographer and videographer
Plan and book honeymoon or organise honeymoon registry
Send save-the-date cards (if using)

4 – 6 months before wedding
Reserve rental equipment, such as tables, chairs and tents
Arrange transportation for the wedding day
Order stationery, including invitations and thank you notes
Register for gifts
Purchase wedding rings
Organise bridesmaid dresses
Choose bonbonniere
Book a room for wedding night

4 months
Discuss details of menu with caterer
Discuss service with celebrant
Choose readings for ceremony
Write your wedding vows, if you choose
Try out make up and hairstyle
Mail invitations

1-2 months
Buy guest book
Print programs, if needed
Register for marriage (must be completed 1 month prior to wedding)
If you intend to change your name, prepare the necessary documents
Contact local newspapers about publishing wedding announcement
Have final dress fitting with shoes, accessories and lingerie
Begin seating plan and write place cards
Notify caterer of final guest count
Write toasts for wedding reception
Break in wedding shoes at home

1 week before wedding
Pick up dress or have it delivered
Confirm final details with caterer
Confirm honeymoon arrangements and give your itinerary to a friend or family member in case of emergency
Pack for honeymoon

1 day before wedding
Confirm transportation arrangements for ceremony and reception
Have manicure and pedicure
Rehearse ceremony
Hold rehearsal dinner; give gifts to wedding party. If you choose, give gifts to parents to thank them for their support

The wedding day
HAVE FUN!

SMART WEDDING

OTHER USEFUL WEB LINKS

UK Wedding planners
http://www.ukawp.com/index.php

Beauty and Make up info
http://www.makeup411.com/

Wedding Jewellery
http://www.springdream.com/

Party Supplies
http://www.ForYourParty.com

Bridal sewing advice
http://www.sewdeb.com/

Shoes
http://www.chineselaundry.com/

Wording and verse for invitations & ceremony
http://www.verseit.com/

Paper & Stationery
http://www.paper-source.com/

Learn to dance online
http://www.bustamove.com/

Custom made heart shapes candy and sweets
http://www.customhearts.com/

Don't want to write that speech?
http://www.free-wedding-speeches.com/

All the information you need to be a best man
http://www.thebestman.com/

Current discount coupons and codes for various supplier websites
http://www.CurrentCodes.com

Celebrity wedding database
http://www.lovetripper.com/bridalstars/wedding-database/database-index.html